# READING AT UNIVERSITY

# READING AT UNIVERSITY
## A Guide for Students

Gavin J. Fairbairn
Susan A. Fairbairn

OPEN UNIVERSITY PRESS
Maidenhead · Philadelphia

Open University Press
McGraw-Hill Education
McGraw-Hill House
Shoppenhangers Road
Maidenhead
Berkshire
England
SL6 2QL

email: equiries@openup.co.uk
world wide web: www.openup.co.uk

and
325 Chestnut Street
Philadelphia, PA 19106, USA

First published 2001

A catalogue record of this book is available from the British Library

ISBN   0 335 20385 X (pb)    0 335 20386 8 (hb)

*Library of Congress Cataloging-in-Publication Data*
Fairbairn, Gavin.
    Reading at university: a guide for students / Gavin J. Fairbairn
and Susan A. Fairbairn.
        p.   cm.
    Includes bibliographical references and index.
    ISBN 0-335-20386-8 — ISBN 0-335-20385-X (pbk.)
    1. Reading (Higher education)   2. Study skills.   I. Fairbairn,
Susan.   II. Title.
LB2395.3 .F35 2001
428.4'071'1—dc21

                                                                    00-050155

Typeset in 10/12pt Palatino by Graphicraft Limited, Hong Kong

Printed and bound in Great Britain by
Marston Lindsay Ross International Ltd,
Oxfordshire

*For Mary West with love and thanks for living in the middle of our crazy household*

# Contents

# Preface

In this book we want to talk about reading – and especially about reading as a student. It has arisen from our experience of helping students to develop the study skills and disciplines they need for success. As a result, though the main focus of the book is on reading, we also raise issues and give advice about other aspects of study.

We would like to acknowledge the help of the many students over the years whose problems with reading gave us the idea for this book. We also want to say thank you to Mary West (who may be the oldest copy-editor and proof-reader in regular employment on the planet), to Thomas Fairbairn who is possibly the most demanding copy-editor on the planet, and to Faith Fairbairn who knows some really good jokes, for example, 'What do Alexander the Great and Winnie the Pooh have in common?' (answer on page 194) and who noticed that we had omitted the word 'are' in a sentence that made no sense.

Thanks are also due to our colleagues at the Open University Press who put up with the delays this book suffered because of personal problems that occurred while we were working on it, especially to Shona Mullen and Anita West. Finally, we would like to thank Professor Donna Mead, Head of the School of Care Sciences at the University of Glamorgan, for her continued support.

*Gavin J. Fairbairn*
*Susan A. Fairbairn*

# Acknowledgements

The authors and the publisher wish to thank the following for permission to print previously published material. Extract from *Knots* by R.D. Laing (1970), page 56, reproduced with the permission of Taylor & Francis. 'Slow Reader' (p.13, 12 lines) from *Please Mrs Butler* by Allan Ahlberg (Kestrel 1983). Copyright © Allan Ahlberg 1983. Reprinted by permission of Penguin Books Ltd. Extract from D. Rowe (1983) *Depression: The Way Out of your Prison*, pages 52–3, reprinted by permission of Routledge. Extract from A. Maclean (1993) *The Elimination of Morality: Reflections on Utilitarianism and Bioethics*, pages 5–6, reprinted by permission of Routledge. Extract from G. Hunt (1999) Abortion: why bioethics can have no answer – a personal perspective, *Nursing Ethics*, 6(1): 47–57, reprinted by permission of Arnold.

# An introductory note

## THE IMPORTANCE OF READING AS A STUDENT

Along with writing and reasoning, reading is one of the most important activities in which students have to engage. This is a fact of life. It is also, unfortunately, a fact of life that most students have problems with reading. There always seems to be too much reading to do and never enough time in which to do it. Reading lists are often too long, lecturers give too many obscure references and even if you were simply to follow up your main interests you would soon find (if you have not done so already) that there is too much information to absorb and too little time in which to absorb it. As a result some students form the view that if only they could read faster, things would be better. Perhaps that is why you have opened this book.

Now, of course there are some advantages to getting through the reading you have to do in the shortest time possible, including the fact that it may give you the chance to do something else with the time you save. That is why a book that claimed to teach students to read faster would probably be an instant success.

Despite our belief that this is the case, this is not that book and you will be disappointed if you read it thinking that it is.

## Better readers make more successful students

Though we will say something both about reading skills and about how to read faster, our primary aim is to get you to think more carefully about your reading – about your reasons for reading, about how and where you read, and about what you do as a result of your reading. We want to urge you to take an active and creative approach, engaging with your sources, interrogating them and using them to build the viewpoints that you present in your essays.

We reject the idea that becoming a good reader is simply a matter of developing skills and strategies. Students who wish to become good readers will have to learn to glean information efficiently from what they read; they will also have to learn to interact creatively and critically with it. They will have to become disciplined readers – who form and maintain good habits, and use their time well, employing the skills and strategies they develop. Too often we make poor use of skills that we have developed, for example in driving our cars and in preparing and cooking nutritious food; something similar is true of the ways in which we use our skills as readers.

Our experience has convinced us that with a small amount of effort, most students can become better readers and hence more successful students.

## Who is this book for?

The issues we address are relevant for students of all disciplines; that is why we have tried, where possible, to use wide-ranging examples. In addition, *Reading at University* is aimed at students at all stages – from the senior years of school, through further education to undergraduate and postgraduate levels. However, if you aren't a student, please don't put the book down just yet. Perhaps, though you are not a student, you picked it up because you are less efficient as a reader than you would like to be, and you wondered whether you might pick up some tips that could help you. We think you probably can.

## What's the point of reading as a student?

Along with listening and observation, reading is an important way in which we gain information about the world. It will underpin much of your academic work as a student, just as it underpins (or should underpin) much of the academic life of your lecturers. Academics must read. They must read in order to become and remain aware of their subject, to keep their knowledge and understanding up to date, and to check their work and ideas and research against those of their peers. You will have to read in order to inform yourself about the subjects you are studying and to allow you to adopt a scholarly approach to your written work. By a 'scholarly approach' we mean one in which you relate what you write to what others have written on the same and related topics.

Reading is one of the most important activities in which you will have to engage, and skill in reading is one of the most important that you will need to develop. Actually that isn't quite right. Reading isn't just one skill, it's a set of skills and in *Reading at University* we will be inviting you to think about some of these. Not only that, but reading is not only a matter of skill. It is also a matter of discipline. As is the case with any skill, including writing and the construction and analysis of arguments, unless you take the trouble to use and to practise your skills as a reader, they will never improve, and your reading will be less beneficial than it could be. That is why we believe that the skills and disciplines of reading are worth acquiring and practising, even if it takes some time and effort to do so, because in the long run – like money invested in stocks and shares – they'll pay dividends.

It is because reading is a major part of the activity in which students have to engage that most reputable guides to study skills give at least some space to discussing it. For example, such guides often present a pot pourri of techniques aimed at helping students to read faster and more efficiently. This book also contains guidance about a variety of ways of reading better, as well as tasks which offer you opportunities for developing your skills as a reader. However, we are committed to the idea that there is more to reading better than reading faster and more efficiently. That is why our main aim in this book is to persuade you to change not only the ways in which you read, but also the ways in which you think about your reading.

## Is learning to read better really worth the time and effort?

Perhaps, until you picked up this book, you had never really thought about reading. Like breathing and walking, it may be so much part of your life that you can't remember a time when you couldn't read. Perhaps you have never considered the possibility that you could learn to read better. We want to convince you not only that improving your reading is possible, but that putting in the small amount of time and effort necessary to do so would be worthwhile.

Some students might think it a foolish waste of precious time to engage in the attempt to improve their reading. They are entitled to their opinion, but they are wrong. Just as those who engage in gymnastic activities of various kinds can improve their performance – for example, by making it stronger, faster or more elegant – those who engage in reading can improve their performance by making it more thoughtful and focused, more detailed, rigorous and effective.

When we read for pleasure, the activity of reading is important in itself. In reading fiction, we read in order to gain pleasurable experiences (even when the subject matter in itself is not pleasant) through our ability imaginatively to inhabit a new world – seeing, feeling and hearing new things. When we read academic texts, on the other hand, we are not motivated primarily by the pleasure we gain by doing so. Most academic reading is motivated by the desire to find, understand and absorb information, ideas and arguments.

Focusing, as we do in this book, on the activity of reading rather than on the information that academic texts contain might be likened to focusing on a window rather than on the view to which it gives us access. An even closer analogy would be with a situation in which we focused on a piece of optical equipment such as a microscope, when what we are really interested in are the cells that we wish to bring into sharper focus. The point is that, just as by polishing a window we can make it easier to see what lies beyond, and by polishing and adjusting the lenses on a microscope we can bring into closer focus the object of our attention, so by polishing up and improving our reading skills we can make it easier to access the information that texts contain.

With the increasing emphasis in many universities and colleges on what is euphemistically referred to as 'resource-based learning', the need for students to develop not only skill as readers, but a disciplined approach to reading, has never been more evident. In an earlier book (Fairbairn and Winch 1996) one of us drew attention to the use, by one university, of what it referred to as the 'FOFO' model, by which it aimed to turn students into autonomous learners by giving them responsibility for their own learning. The acronym FOFO arises from the central plank of the model. At an early point in their careeer all students were taught that in researching for their essays and assignments they should 'First Organise and Find Out'. This is good advice which could not only underpin a worthwhile study skills programme but also a worthwhile approach to study. However, cynicism, combined with an unfortunate lack of resources, led many students of this university to give another meaning to the first part of the acronym, which you may imagine, but which we couldn't possibly print in a book of this kind.

The cynicism of the students in the FOFO example is shared by many academic staff, though in their case it relates to what they take to be the unstated motivation of senior managers who they believe embrace student-centred and resource-based learning in order to cut costs. To some extent we share this sceptical view of the reasons that student-directed learning has become popular. However, we also believe strongly that the primary responsibility for getting information into a student's head rests with the student, rather than with those who teach him. The responsibility of lecturers is to motivate and interest students, supporting them in the intellectual work necessary to come to terms with new ideas and information, rather than spoonfeeding them with knowledge which they passively absorb. This has an implication in terms of the ways in which, and the extent to which, we believe that university and college lecturers should guide and direct students in their reading. For example, it inclines us towards the view that the use of 'reading lists' often hinders rather than helps students' development.

Whatever the rationale of the move towards students being given more responsibility for accessing information during their studies, the importance of reading for study is clear. It is even more clear in the case of students studying through distance learning institutions like The Open University, where the primary mode of instruction is the course text, which may be thought of as a series of 'written lectures'. In the case of students in institutions with highly developed IT facilities, significant amounts of teaching and other information may be conveyed or made available via the Internet, which again may involve more reading than a traditional lecturing approach.

Whatever the institution, the course and the approaches to teaching and learning that are adopted, it is clear that the better you are and become at reading, the better. This is true, even though it is commonly argued that reading will become less important as books and traditional academic journals are overtaken by electronic media as the mainstay for academic and intellectual communication, including teaching and the sharing of original research and theoretical developments. Electronic media, including CD ROM and DVD, 'e-books', and the Internet (with its oceans of sometimes high quality information sources – including Internet journals with standards of scholarship that are equivalent to their paper counterparts), are having a major impact in academic life, not least in the way in which courses are delivered. Nonetheless, we feel confident that for the forseeable future the skills and disciplines of reading will be central to students' lives.

The revolution in information technology has affected both the ways in which and the ease with which information can be made accessible, in much the same way as the invention of the printing press and television. It has also provided possibilities for interactive work and learning through on-line discussion and videoconferencing. Finally, the rise of electronic media has made it possible for the written or printed word to be combined with other forms of communication in published academic products. Authors who choose to communicate via, for example, the Internet can now illustrate and argue for their conclusions, using not only photographs but also film and sound. However, as with older communications technologies such as print, film and television, we should exercise caution, rigorously assessing the quality of information available.

In any case, in spite of the rise of the Internet as a source of information, it has not yet taken away the centrality of reading as a way of accessing information for academic purposes. Indeed, unless we move to a technology in which most information is conveyed aurally or pictorially or by some yet to be invented system (perhaps ECMDDT – Electronic Computer to Mind Direct Data Transfer?), reading – whether from hard copy in the form of printed material, or from a computer screen – will remain highly significant.

### But aren't most students already competent readers?

By the time they get to university or college, most students will already be reasonably competent readers. For example, as well as being able to decode print in a way that allows you to guess how unknown words will sound when spoken, you will be able to use clues supplied by the text to guess at the meanings of words with which you are unfamiliar, and to infer meanings that are implied though not stated. It is likely also that you will be able to predict at least some of what is coming as you read and that, to some extent, you will be able to infer meanings and ideas from print without reading every word, though you may revert to doing so when you come across material with which you are unfamiliar, especially if new and complex-sounding or specialized words are used.

Unfortunately, in spite of their experience as readers, or perhaps even because of it, most students will have gaps in their reading skills, just as they will have gaps in other basic study skills – in writing and in time management, for example. This is likely to be true of you just as much as it is of your fellow students. Why else would you be reading, in however superficial a way, a book about ways of improving your reading at university?

Between us we have studied a frighteningly diverse set of sub-jects at either undergraduate or postgraduate level including geo-logy, geography, maths, chemistry, physics, biology, psychology, music, primary and special education, educational research methods, statistics, computer studies and philosophy. By referring to our time as students in such a wide range of areas, we do not intend to draw attention to how well educated we are – but to give some credibility to our claim to know that reading has immense importance in the study of most, if not all, academic subjects. Not only that, but we think we can remember enough about our own experience as students to allow us to enter imaginatively into the lives of student readers from a range of disciplines.

## GETTING TO KNOW THIS BOOK

In this book, though our main aim is to talk about reading, what we have to say will impinge, also, on other study skills including time management, note taking, writing and the assessment of arguments, because all of these will be intermingled in your life as a student.

### What do we hope to achieve?

We want to give you some help in becoming the best and most effective reader that you can be, in order that you can get as much benefit out of your studies as possible, while having the maximum possible amount of time left for all the other things you have to do and want to do.

We address a wide range of concerns and needs that are common to all students. One of these you are likely to share with most students throughout history – from the time when students literally went to universities to 'read' for a degree because, along with religious centres, they were the only places where books were to be found in quantity. We are referring to the concern that most students have about the relatively small amount of time they are able to devote to reading the mountains of material that they are either told they must read, or decide they need to read. Quite apart from the fact that there is too much written in relation to almost everything to allow you to hope ever to read even a tiny fraction of what has been written about your subject, other activities are also important and need to be given time – writing assignments and reports, eating and drinking, listening to music and talking to friends, to name but a few. The time that you can make available for reading will clearly never be enough. You will have to learn to live with this fact, without letting it depress you. Bear in mind that what really matters isn't how much you read, but the use that you make of the reading that you do.

As a student you will have to read in a variety of ways, at a range of levels and for many different purposes. We want to help you to develop as a reader who is able to approach a range of reading tasks in a disciplined way, equipped with appropriate and helpful strategies. We will do this both by sharing ideas and by inviting you to try out some suggestions for approaches that we believe can help you.

## How to read this book

How you go about reading this book will depend upon the ways in which you have developed as a reader so far. If you have already developed sophisticated skills and strategies as a reader of academic texts, you may be reading this because you are approaching the book in a fairly systematic way to assess its relevance. If this is the case, you may have tried to gain a feel for the level at which it is pitched, by first looking at the blurb on the back cover, the contents list and the index, then at the beginnings and ends of its main parts, and at sections with headings that caught your attention – such as 'How to read this book'. Such a procedure, which we discuss in more detail later, will often help you to decide whether a book is worth borrowing or even buying. As a result of such scrutiny, you may have formed the view that this introduction offers a brief and easy overview that would be worth reading in detail, before proceeding to parts of the book that seem to address your particular concerns.

On the other hand, you might have begun reading the book at the beginning – in the expectation that you will then read through from cover to cover, in the hope that you might gain some ideas about how to improve your reading. If this is the case, we suggest that you should turn to our discussion of ways of approaching unfamiliar texts and of deciding whether or not they are worth-while reading (see pages 90–6).

## Tasks

Scattered throughout the book you will find a number of tasks. Some are designed to help you to get to know yourself as a reader. They invite you to think about aspects of your experience of reading, and the ways in which you read. This should help you to decide which aspects of your reading habits and approaches are most in need of attention. Other tasks give you the opportunity to try out or practise strategies and skills that you may find helpful.

How much time you commit to these tasks is up to you. However, we hope you will be willing to give at least a little thought to the questions we raise, and a little time to the exercises we propose, because we believe that you will find them helpful in developing as a skilled, disciplined and thoughtful reader. Some tasks ask you to do things away from this book, using material to which you have access in your home, or in your institutional or local library. Others ask you to work with material that we supply. Most of the exercises have no definitive 'answer'; however, we offer comments about some, and possible responses to others. Sometimes these comments and responses are to be found towards the end of the book, because we want to encourage you to undertake the exercise without first looking at what we have said about it; where this is the case, you will be directed to the appropriate page.

## Language and style

There are, finally, a few things that we should tell you about the language and style we have adopted in writing this book.

### Essays or assignments?

In referring to the writing that students have to undertake, we use the terms 'assignment' and 'essay' interchangeably, even though an essay is a particular form of assignment and one in which some students will rarely be asked to engage. We have done this because the essay is a very common form of assignment and we wanted to avoid cumbersome references to 'essays, reports, and assignments of other kinds'. And so whenever you read a reference to essays and/or assignments, you should take us to be referring to whatever forms of written assessment you are expected to complete.

## Style

Although this is a book about reading, we recognize that the reading you will do as a student will inevitably be linked closely to your writing. And so from time to time we take the opportunity to share some of what we believe about academic writing style. We hope that we can influence you into developing a style that, as far as is possible, emulates the good academic writers whose work, with any luck, you will read during your studies, and, at a minimum, avoids the pitfalls of many of the poor academic writers whose work you will inevitably come across.

As a result of our beliefs in the value of simplicity, the style in which we have written this book is probably different from that of many if not most of the books you will read as a student. We are discursive and at times anecdotal, couching advice in discussions of our experience both as teachers and as students, because we believe strongly that useful learning often comes about through the sharing of experience. Unlike many academic writers, we have tried to avoid difficult words and jargon where possible, with the aim of making the book as easy to read, as inviting and non-intimidating as possible. We wanted to tell you this because we would hate you to form the impression that just because we try to avoid using difficult words where possible, we can't be real academics like the authors of many of the articles in academic journals and books with which you will come into contact, and some of which you will read.

Obviously as a student you will have to attend to the stylistic requirements of your subject and to the demands that your lecturers make. However, we strongly recommend that you should take careful note of which authors are most successful in engaging and communicating with you as a reader, and that, where possible, you should try to incorporate elements of their style into your work.

Learning to spot good and poor academic style can also help you in developing a feel for texts that are worth reading and skill in spotting those that are worth leaving well alone. Given the limited time you can spend on reading, it is generally better (all things being equal – for example, the texts in question being of similar significance, to the best of your knowledge) to use your time in reading texts that communicate easily and well, than to waste it on texts that are so poorly written that you can barely understand what they are about.

---

### Portfolios of good and bad academic writing

You may find it helpful to compile a portfolio of examples of good academic writing that you come across. You will be able to spot good academic writing, because it will be successful in communicating ideas and arguments – however complex. Use a loose leaf file to catalogue and store photocopied examples of such writing, which may comprise anything from individual paragraphs or pages, through to complete chapters from books, or journal articles. Alongside each item insert a few notes about why you think it is successful. For example, is it successful because it uses short sentences or simple words; because it is written in the first person, or because it largely avoids jargon?

It is also worth compiling a collection of examples of bad academic writing, including stuff that is unreadable and fails to communicate anything other than the impression that its author must be very, very intelligent if she knows what she is talking about. Catalogue and store examples of bad academic writing that you come across, again with a few notes about why they are unsuccessful in communicating.

---

Whether we have been successful in writing simply and directly, in a way that makes what we want to say as easy for you to follow as possible, is for you to judge. Whatever you decide, we stick by our belief that simplicity is generally a virtue in academic writing, whether it is aimed at professional or student academics.

## First, second or third person?

You will perhaps find us rather promiscuous in the way that we seem to drift between the use of the first, second and third person. In other words, although much of the time, identifying ourselves directly as those who are speaking, we adopt the first person, using expressions such as 'We believe that...'; 'We hope that you might...' and 'To return for a moment to what we said about...', we also sometimes write (more distantly some would say) in the third person, using sentences such as 'It is because reading is a major part of the activity in which students have to engage, that most reputable guides to study...'. Lastly, we sometimes address you directly using the second person, in sentences like 'However, if you aren't a student, please don't put the book down just yet.'

Despite the prejudices of those academics who believe that the third person and the third person alone should be used in academic work, the first person is often used very effectively in the rigorous development of arguments. Nonetheless you will find that academic work is most often written in the third person. Indeed, even in disciplines such as psychology, education and nursing where the first person is used by many authors, its use is often frowned upon. Depending on your subject and the personal views of your lecturers, you may find that you are required to adopt the third person in your written work.

## Gender

Finally, we should say something about the ways in which we have attempted to address the offence that gender-specific language causes some people. In other words, we should tell you how we have chosen to avoid the overuse of the pronouns 'he', 'his' and 'him', which used to characterize most non-fiction writing.

Some authors attempt to deal with the problem by always using plural forms of pronouns: 'them', 'they' and 'their', even when they are referring to individuals; we have rejected this strategy because we find the results stylistically offensive. For similar reasons, we have chosen not to enter into the habit of always referring to 'he/she', 'him/her' or 'his/her' (or 'her/him', 'her/his' or 'she/he' – or, even worse, 's/he'). Nonetheless, be-cause we want to recognize that there are both female and male people in the world, and because we want to avoid offending anyone who may be lying in wait, waiting to be offended, we have tried to be consistent in the use of the following strategy, unless its use would cause confusion.

When we are referring to specific individuals we use pronouns that are appropriate to their gender. However, when we are re-ferring to non-identified students we usually refer to them using male pronouns, and in general, when we are referring to non-identified academics or writers, we use female pronouns. Finally, where individuals to whom we refer are neither students nor academics/writers, we try our best to avoid the overuse of either female or male pronouns. Although this strategy may have some odd results – including the possibility that it might induce a casual reader into thinking that we believe that most students are men while most academics and writers are women – this seems less important to us than the attempt to avoid offence while maintaining some kind of stylistic integrity.

# PART 1: Thinking about reading and about yourself as a reader

Toby was neu years old and had a holl of oun ret. His great-est vilt was a tecture called **Fred**. Toby lev Fred each yak and gave him holls of welt to pock, he even beck him cutch peus when he could get them from his kult. Fred was mump enough to pell in the gelt of Toby's fing and remp his juges.

(Raban 1982)

In Part 1 we invite you to think about yourself as a reader, exploring the ways in which you read and reflecting on how you came to read like this. We ask you to consider whether your reading skills and disciplines and the ways in which you think about and approach reading are as helpful as they might be.

## THINKING ABOUT READING

What is reading? You may think that this is a foolish question to ask you – because, for example, you've been a reader for so long that it's obvious you know what reading is. Learning to read is one of the first things children do in school and, at a basic level, schools do a good job in teaching most children to read. None-theless, the question of what reading is, is not simple. Reading is a complex set of different activities requiring a range of skills. Reflecting on this complexity and on the range of ways in which you can read should help you to become a better reader.

Most often when we talk of 'learning to read' we are talking about the early stages of reading – the first stumbling steps that we take as children in decoding print and beginning to under-stand that those odd marks on the page carry meaning. There is a good deal of disagreement about the best way of teaching chil-dren to read, which is arguably rooted in different ways of think-ing about reading. For example, a teacher who emphasizes the ability to work out what words will sound like, and encourages children to 'sound out' new words letter by letter or syllable by syllable, will have a different conception of reading than one who uses the 'look and say' approach, which emphasizes the recogni-tion of whole words. Of course, recognizing the advantages of doing so, good teachers in primary schools have embraced both emphases for many years and nowadays teachers in all state schools are expected to do so.

There are even bigger differences between those who utilize these approaches to the teaching of reading and those, in recent years, who embraced the idea that most if not all children could learn to read simply through exposure to 'real books' and lots of guided and supported opportunities to engage with them.[1] Though this works well for some children, it does not work for others. For example, although as a small child our son Thomas was far from starved of reading material, or of opportunities to 'catch' reading from adults who read with him, he did not learn to read naturally – as we had grown to expect he would. Inter-estingly, when he was little, Thomas developed bizarre ideas about the nature of the letters which comprise our typed and written script, that mitigated against his simply 'catching' read-ing, because they made the complex task of learning to read even more difficult. For example, at one point he thought that there were subtle differences in meaning between 'a's that looked

---

1 The expression 'real books' refers to books that are not published specifically for use in teaching children to read. Such books might be picture books, story books, or non-fiction books.

different – for example, 'a'; 'a', '**a**', 'a' and '**a**', though he could not work out what they were. When he eventually realized that what mattered was only the ways in which letters are combined, rather than their form, he took off and quickly became a capable reader.

No matter how long ago you learned to read, the ways in which you did so may have influenced both your attitudes to reading and the ways in which you read. We have both worked in primary schools and thus know something of the excellence that is often attained by teachers, especially in the early years. However, we also know that reading has casualties who leave school at best semi-literate, and many more who leave with reading skills that are less good than they might be. We have known many people who, at least partly as a result of unsupportive, unempathic and uninspiring early teaching, find difficulties with reading when they are students. One of the least helpful things that can happen is when a teacher fails to treat children as individuals who differ from one another in their needs as beginning readers. When this happens a programmatic approach to the reading will be adopted, which will suit some but not all children. It may put others off for life.

Strange though it may seem, in some schools even children who can already read have to go through the whole process of 'learning to read'. It is almost as if their teachers believe that there is an apprenticeship that must be served in becoming a reader, and a prescribed number of simple books that must be laboriously 'read', before a newly qualified reader's competence can be trusted. Children who learn to read early – whether at home or in school – may thus be held back by teachers who do not recognize their competence, and make them stay with simple books in school, when they are already reading more complex books independently and with good understanding at home. For example, in spite of the fact that our daughter Faith learned to read very quickly, her teacher persisted in sending her home with inappropriate 'reading books', even when we pointed out that she was reading more difficult books independently at home. What was worse, Faith insisted on reading her school 'reading' books to us in the robotic 'Jan-et-and-Pe-ter-go-to-the-park. It-is-sun-ny' way that characterizes many children's early experience of vocalizing the sounds represented by print. When we asked her why she read her school books to us like this, she explained that this was how she had to read for 'Miss'.

When, on page 26, we invite you to think about your history as a reader, it may be interesting to try to recall whether, when you were learning to read, emphasis was laid on the ability to recognize individual letters or groups of letters and the sounds they make, or rather on the recognition of whole words. Perhaps the person who taught you to read emphasized the ability to guess at the meanings conveyed by a piece of text, using clues offered by illustrations and what you already knew about the story?

---

**Defining reading**                                      *Task 1.1*

Write down your own view of what reading is, in a few lines. Bear in mind that there is no right or wrong answer. We're not asking for a well-honed definition; just give a little thought to what you think reading is.

---

It is quite likely that you have never given much thought to the processes of reading. However, bringing your ideas about reading into your conscious awareness is a first step towards identifying places where you can improve your skills and hence performance.

## So what is reading?

At the most basic level, reading is sometimes thought to consist of translating symbols on a page, or nowadays on a computer screen, into sounds, in what is sometimes referred to as 'barking at print'. Some people would argue that this isn't reading at all. We wouldn't agree. However, it is clear that there is more to reading than merely being able to perform the neat trick of vocalizing the sounds that are represented by the symbols with which we record speech and thought. It also comprises a range of other skills, including those that allow us to decide from context what is intended by words that can have more than one meaning, and to grasp from a glance at a chunk of print the general meaning intended, without reading each individual word.

Muslim readers will probably remember learning to read the Qu'ran (Koran) from Arabic script, in classes at the mosque. We gather from Muslim friends that, traditionally, Muslim children learn to read the Qu'ran in Arabic when they are small, even though they are considered to be too young for proper comprehension. The first experience many Muslim children have of decoding print thus has nothing at all to do with meaning. As a result, some Muslim children who are learning to read English as a second or third language initially find it difficult to understand that this new kind of reading is about extracting meaning.

Some people would claim that reading is to writing as listening is to speaking – in the sense that whereas writing and speaking are ways in which we communicate information and ideas, reading and listening are ways in which we receive them. We strongly disagree with this idea. Human communication is always a two-way process. Most of the time when we are speaking and writing we will be engaging with things that others have already said or written; and most of the time when we are reading and listening we will be relating the ideas that writers and speakers present to our previous knowledge and experience. In a way this is obvious – after all, how can you possibly understand what you read and hear, if you do not make use of what you already know in doing so? However, it is worth realizing that the more conscious you are of the need to use what you know when you read and listen, and the more actively you try to relate what you read and hear to what you already know, the more efficient you will become as a reader and listener. We address this idea in more detail in Part 4, where we urge you to make the conscious effort always to read actively.

## GROWING AS A READER

If you are to make good use of your reading you may have to throw off childlike reading habits that stem, perhaps, from a time when your teachers expected you to read out loud. Many people retain remnants of early reading habits in their reading as adults. For example, when they are reading fiction, the compulsion to read every word may overpower them, even though, when they are reading non-fiction, they manage to adopt a range of different approaches. For others the difference will go in the opposite direction, so that although they feel almost duty bound to read every word in a non-fiction text, they find it entirely natural to skip merrily past whole chunks of fictional texts, in pursuit of the bones of a storyline.

Surprising though it may seem, some aspects of the teaching of reading that has gone on and may still go on in schools arguably contribute to the development of unhelpful ways of approaching text that can be found in students. Let us illustrate what we are talking about, using an amusing example taken from a book about the assessment of reading by Raban (1982) that you will have noticed at the beginning of Part 2. Can you remember the kind of exercise that she is caricaturing?

---

**Comprehension by Raban (1982)**                          *Task 1.2*

Read Raban's passage and try answering her questions. Then try it on a friend along with some extra questions of your own. You might, for example, ask a question about the peus that Toby beck Fred to cutch. You might also like to try writing your own passage and questions in the same vein.

---

Toby was neu years old and had a holl of oun ret. His greatest vilt was a tecture called Fred. Toby lev Fred each yak and gave him holls of welt to pock, he even beck him cutch peus when he could get them from his kult. Fred was mump enough to pell in the gelt of Toby's fing and remp his juges.

*Answer these questions in full sentences:*

1 How old was Toby?
2 What did Toby have a holl of?
3 What did Toby do to Fred each yak?
4 What did Toby give to Fred?
5 Why was Fred able to pell in the gelt of Toby's fing?
6 What did Fred remp?

(Raban 1982, p.7)

There is no doubt that if you are able to read this book, you are able to read Raban's passage about Toby and his vilt, Fred; or at least you will be able to read it in the sense of saying it aloud. Not only that, however – you will also be able to answer Raban's questions about the passage, even though you do not understand a word of it. So, for example, without knowing what 'oun ret' is, you will be able to work out that Toby had a holl of it, and though you have no idea what Toby's 'fing' is or where it is to be found, you will know that Fred was able to pell in its gelt, because he was 'mump enough'.

The reason you will be able to do all of this is that (whether you are aware of it or not) you have a sophisticated understanding of the way in which our language works, which includes knowledge about the functions of different kinds of words. And so, although you can only guess at what they mean, you know that 'lev' and 'pell' are verbs, and that 'vilt', 'kult' and 'tecture' are nouns; you are likely, also, to be able to guess that while a 'yak' is a measure of time, a 'holl' is a measure that is used in relation to materials such as 'oun ret' (or perhaps 'ret') and 'welt', whatever they are.

Raban's example demonstrates that a general understanding of the ways in which language works can allow us to answer some questions about a piece of text without any knowledge of what it means. You are unlikely ever to be required to answer such questions as a student, though you will have answered screeds of them as a school pupil. However, Raban's example draws attention to dangers that exist when you come across texts that you do not understand, in connection with your work as a student. For example, it demonstrates clearly that knowing something about how language works will often allow you to write about a piece of text as if you understand it, without having the foggiest notion of what it is about.

Many students fall into the dangerous habit of trying, in their work, to persuade their lecturers and tutors that they know and understand things that they do not. This is particularly common among students who are fond of technical language and jargon, and who have formed the deluded idea that its use necessarily conveys an aura of sophistication and the impression that one has mastered one's topic. Such students are likely to believe that writing as if they know and understand the texts they read, even when they do not, will persuade their lecturers that they are worthy of decent marks; it is as if they do not expect to be caught out. They are putting their trust in the naïve belief that lecturers never 'really read' essays. Unfortunately this is not true – at least some lecturers do read essays carefully!

Of course, not all students who write in the kind of ways that we are referring to, do so in order deliberately to deceive their lecturers about what they know. Some do it because they are unwilling to own up to uncertainty about what they read, even when they come across complex and difficult ideas for the first time. A similar unwillingness to own up to ignorance is also encountered in lectures and seminars, when students often fail to ask lecturers to explain things, for fear of looking foolish. The experience of the intellectual and emotional tangles in which many people become involved, in trying to avoid exposing their ignorance, was brilliantly summed up by the Scottish psychiatrist R.D. Laing (1970):

There is something I don't know
    that I am supposed to know.
I don't know *what* it is I am supposed to know,
    and yet I am supposed to know,
and I feel I look stupid
    if I seem both not to know it
        and not know *what* it is I don't know.
Therefore I pretend I know it.

Extract from *Knots* (p.56)

Do you ever pretend to know what you don't know? Or to understand what you don't understand? When you are reading for your coursework or essays, and you come across things that you don't understand, do you ever persuade yourself to believe that all that matters in your essays and exam answers is that you should look as if you have read the right things – or the right kind of things? Or are you brave enough – wise enough – to ask others to help you when you come across passages, or even whole texts, that are beyond your comprehension?

The temptation to feign knowledge and expertise is present even for postgraduate students. One of us recently heard a professor of law talking about a PhD thesis he had examined in which the candidate referred to some literature about which she seemed to have little understanding. This was a bad mistake on her part, since, to her great bad luck, it was literature in which this professor had a developed interest. By referring to this material in a way that suggested that she had used it in developing her thesis, even though her knowledge of it was slight, she thus laid a trap for herself.

As a student, your job is to learn, even at the expense of admitting that you don't know, and the sooner you learn to admit that at times you don't know and understand, the better. Pretending that you understand what your lecturers are going on about and what you are reading in books, when you do not, is just about the most stupid thing that you can do as a student; while honestly admitting to ignorance, thus opening yourself to the possibility of learning, is probably the most important thing you can learn to do.

**Old habits die hard**

Perhaps you feel insulted that we have been talking about the need to avoid reading in ways that hark back to the days when you were just beginning to read. You may believe that you are far beyond that kind of thing. However, our experience suggests that many students are stuck in ways of thinking about reading and approaches to reading that belong to their early life, or revert at times to ways of reading in which they engaged as children. For example, they may read every word or feel as if they are somehow cheating if they do not; and at times they may read books from cover to cover (or attempt to do so), rather than reading them in whatever way and in whatever order suits them best. Some people find themselves vocalizing[2] when they come across words with which they are unfamiliar, or when they are reading material that is complex and difficult to understand.

There is obvious merit in being able to work out how words sound when we first come across them. For example, it can help us to absorb them more readily into both our active and our

---

2 'Vocalizing' can, of course, happen silently inside our heads or under our breath, when it is often called 'sub-vocalizing'.

passive vocabulary,[3] and when necessary it can allow us to look them up in a dictionary. Consider, for example, what happens when you read the following:

> He wrote in a style that clouded meaning and seemed to be aimed at obfuscation rather than clarity. Indeed his writing style was so full of idiosagacity that others could rarely understand what he wrote.

How did you cope with that remarkable word 'idiosagacity'? For example, did you read it with an immediate sense of its meaning or did you guess at what it means because you know what 'obfuscatory' means or because you know what both the prefix 'idio' and the word 'sagacious' mean? Did you perhaps guess at its meaning because you understood the previous sentence? Or did you, rather, hover over it, sounding it out syllable by syllable: id-io-sag-a-ci-ty in a desperate attempt to get some sense of what it might be intended to convey? Do you even believe that it is a real word?

Ask yourself whether and when you hear words in your head as you read. Does it happen all the time? Some of the time? Never? Try, as you read texts of various kinds, to be conscious of whether you are reading individual words or groups of words, indeed whether you are conscious of words at all. For some people, the sound of the words that they read is a real and important part of the experience of reading, especially, but not only, when they are reading fiction. For example, a friend recently told us about an autobiographical book she had just read, which demanded to be read with an Irish accent; her claim was that there was no other way in which she could have approached it. In this case, what is in question is not language but dialect and accent, and our friend clearly felt that the most authentic way of approaching the experiences that the author wished to convey was to meet the text in a voice in which he might have spoken it.

---

3 Our *active vocabulary* is the set of words that we know well enough to allow us to use them in constructing the things we say and write, while our *passive vocabulary* comprises the much larger set of words that we understand when we come across them, but which we are not yet able to use.

In contrast to the experience of those who find that they are conscious of every word when they read fiction, many people find, especially but not exclusively when they are reading fiction, that when they 'get into' the text they seem to be aware of meanings, sounds and pictures, even smells and feelings, without any conscious awareness of the words used to convey them. Some people find something similar happening when they are reading academic texts, especially when the authors have succeeded in communicating clearly.

Sometimes people who usually read without giving any thought to the sound of the words, find themselves reading more slowly and 'subvocalizing' when they are trying to read material that they consider to be of great importance, even if there is nothing particularly difficult about either the content or the vocabulary. Perhaps they think, whether consciously or unconsciously, that by reading like this they will be able to absorb every word – to soak up its importance, understanding and internalizing every bit of meaning.

Reading slowly, listening to the sounds of words as well as to their meanings, can be beneficial – when you are in control of it. For example, it can help you to absorb meaning by focusing attention in a detailed way on what an author is trying to communicate. However, hearing the sounds of words when you read can be a handicap. For example, it can reduce the speed with which you read, which might in turn reduce your ability to absorb meaning. Barnes (1995) points out that '. . . you stand a better chance of remembering the first half of a sentence if you read quickly enough to reach the second half' (p.53). The point, of course, is that if you read too slowly it is more difficult to get a broad grasp of what is being said, because you will often need to know what the end of a sentence is, before you can fully understand the beginning. Rereading a sentence or paragraph or page rather quickly several times will often be more useful than reading really slowly.

Reading slowly can also lead to lapses in attention and consequent negative effects on the making of meaning, as the reader lapses back into earlier habits and begins simply to decode words, silently barking at print. At its most extreme, this problem can result in the reader merely looking at print, rather than engaging with it at any level.

## THINKING ABOUT YOURSELF AS READER

As a first step to improving your skills and disciplines as a reader, we want to invite you to think a little about your reading history. Later at various points we will invite you to reflect on your strengths and weaknesses, and hence on aspects of your reading that can usefully be improved.

---

### How did you become the reader that you are?   *Task 1.3*

Think about your career as a reader. Try to remember something about the journey you have made as a reader, from your first tottering steps in trying, as a novice, to understand and decode print, to the way you are today.

Can you remember learning to read? Or do you feel as if you were born with this ability?

Did reading come easily to you, or did you struggle? If you struggled, try to remember something about your experience – how did it feel?

What messages did you receive from your teachers when you were beginning to read? Were they supportive or unsupportive? How do you think their input affected your growth as a reader?

What did you learn about reading, at home? Did the adults with whom you lived as a child encourage you or put you off? Were you surrounded by books that were read?

Did you enjoy reading as a child? What did you read? School books? Comics? Books from the library? Books you were bought? Books you bought yourself?

Can you remember your favourite three books from childhood?

Did you use a torch to read under the bed clothes at night when you were supposed to be asleep?

Can you remember being taught reading skills, after you had learned to read? For example, were you taught to skim and scan text?

How did you get on? Was it easy or difficult to recall your history as a reader? Did you find yourself remembering things you'd forgotten? Some people recall learning to read as one of the most exciting times of their life, while others remember it as a time of misery.

One of us, who was reading by the time she was three, cannot recall anything at all about the process of learning to read. The other can remember the Janet and John[4] stage vividly, but then his memory of reading jumps forward to the time towards the end of primary school, when every week he and a friend (where are you now Norman Westbrook?) used to walk three miles to the library in Colinton village on the edge of Edinburgh, to continue reading their way through the children's collection.

In trying to recall your history as a reader, did you come across memories about being taught to do anything other than decode words, or perhaps about how to use alphabetical order to look things up in dictionaries and other alphabetical lists? For example, were you taught how to use reference books to find information? Interestingly, there is now some emphasis in primary schools in the UK, on the development of a range of reading skills that may go far beyond those you learned as a child. Among these is skill in assessing books. A couple of years ago, for example, one of us asked our daughter Faith (then aged 9) how she would decide whether a story book was worth taking out of the library. Her answer went like this:

> Well first I'd look at the title to see whether it interested me and then at the picture on the front cover because sometimes pictures help but not always because sometimes they just put interesting pictures on to get you interested. Then I'd look at the blurb – you know, on the back cover, to see what it said about the book. After that I'd look inside – at

---

4 We are referring to a stage, in many of the reading schemes that have been popular in the UK over the last forty or fifty years, where the language used is rather stilted, and characterized by sentences such as 'Janet and John are in the park. They play with a ball. It is red.' Sometimes the characters have different names which, with the advent of political correctness and multicultural awareness, might include names like Mario, Abdul and Sita. One such series of books features the archetypal heroine and hero Janet and John whose adventures take them to exciting places like school and parks, shops and back gardens.

the contents list, to see what the chapters were about and then I'd flick through reading little bits to see if I wanted to read it.[5]

Faith clearly has a developed strategy for deciding which story books to read; she learned it in school. Do you have such a strategy? If you do, how did you come to have it? Did you develop it yourself? Or were you taught it as a child?

Sometimes when people begin to think about their history as readers they discover lost memories about messages they received as beginning readers – messages that might well be influencing their reading as adult students. For example, someone who has difficulties in getting through reading might recall being told they weren't trying hard enough when, as a child, they were slower than their friends. The devastation that might be caused to a child by being labelled as a 'slow reader' can be directly experienced simply by reading aloud Allan Ahlberg's wonderful poem *Slow Reader* (1984). Please try it.

**Slow Reader**

I - am - in - the - slow
read - ers - group - my - broth
er - is - in - the - foot
ball - team - my - sis - ter
is - a - ser - ver - my
lit - tle - broth - er - was
a wise - man - in - the
in - fants - Christ - mas - play
I - am - in - the - slow
read - ers - group - that - is
all - I - am - in - I
hate - it.

Were you a slow reader? Or were you, like one of us, a child who had a reading age of 14 when she was 7?

---

5 When, recently, we asked how she would assess a book that wasn't a story book, she said, 'Do you mean an information book?' and proceeded to talk, among other things, in terms of skimming chunks and of scanning for particular words in which she is interested; we haven't yet discovered whether she was taught this or caught it from us.

**What are you like as a reader?**

Now that you've thought a little about your history as a reader, take some time to think about yourself as a reader now – for example, about the range of material you read, when you read, and the different ways in which you read. Notice that we are not asking you to focus specifically on academic reading at the moment – we shall come to that in Part 2.

---

**What are you like as a reader?**                    *Task 1.4*

---

Do you enjoy reading? Or is it a chore? Do you sometimes enjoy it and sometimes hate it? What's the difference between reading that you like, and reading that you don't like?

If you don't enjoy reading, why don't you enjoy it?

Do you think you're a good reader? If so, make a list of your strengths. On the other hand, if you think you aren't a good reader, try to list the problems you have. (Then try listing your strengths as a reader, because if you are managing to read this, you must have some.)

Do you read for pleasure? Or do you only read in connection with your coursework?

If you read for pleasure, what do you read? (Novels? Non-fiction books? Magazines? websites?).

If you don't read for pleasure, why don't you? Is it that you don't enjoy reading? Or do you find it difficult? Is it hard to find the time?

What do you find easiest to read? What do you find most difficult to read? What is the difference between things you find easy to read and those you find difficult?

Do you ever have several books 'on the go' at the same time? If so, why? Is it because it allows you to dot from one to the other, thus maintaining some level of interest in a number of different topics at the same time?

Do you talk to other people about what you read? To what extent is your choice of reading material influenced by others?

Which books do you manage to finish reading? And which do you never get through, no matter how hard you try? Do books that you finish and books that you abandon part way through demand to be read in different ways?

When you don't finish reading a book do you feel guilty? If not, why not? If yes, why yes?

We all differ from one another in the things we read, the ways we read, the time we give to reading and the extent to which we share our reading with others. For some people reading is little more than a skill that they employ when necessary. For others it is almost a substitute for social life, in which the characters in fictional books are like friends who have come to stay. This is particularly common for those who reread a favourite book many times. How big a part of your life do the characters that inhabit fictional books become for you? And how real do the characters that inhabit academic books – the theories and arguments and hypotheses they contain – become for you?

Some people would never dream of discussing the things they read with friends while, for others, reading is very much a social activity. One of our friends frequently manages, even in short conversations, to let us know what she is reading at the moment, in the same way that other people might talk about the latest movie they have seen. Another friend is part of a reading group, the members of which meet regularly to discuss books (usually, but not exclusively, novels) that they have jointly decided to read. Members of such groups enjoy the opportunity to explore ideas, images and emotions evoked by the books they read, thus enriching their understanding of those books and allowing them to develop their critical faculties as they share their views and opinions. You might like to consider setting up such a group as part of your study programme. This might seem like a naff idea – after all, students aren't meant to sit round discussing work; they're supposed to sit around talking about music and sex and movies and travelling – anything but work. On the other hand, the idea of a few pals sitting round once a fortnight, or once a month, with a bottle of wine and a book, or even an article, that you have all agreed to read and discuss, doesn't seem totally unattractive to us. We think that sharing reading with friends can be really helpful, and in Part 9 we talk about some other ways in which you might do so.

## How do you read?

Let's now look more closely at some aspects of your reading, remembering that for the moment we do not want you to focus specifically on academic reading. We hope that by consciously focusing on your reading habits – how, where and when you read – you might be in a better position to change your reading for the better. Your current approaches to reading may seem inefficient once you think carefully about them.

---

**How do you read?**                                        *Task 1.5*

Do you always read in the same way? Or do you employ different strategies, depending on what you are reading?

For example, do you read differently when you are reading fiction than when you are reading non-fiction?

Do you read books in the same way as you read magazines or newspapers?

Does the way you read books depend on what you hope to get from them?

Do you always read novels from beginning to end? Do you sometimes skip back to check details about the plot and characters?

What else do you do while you are reading? For example, do you listen to music? If you do, are you conscious of the results of doing so? Does accompanying noise prevent your mind wandering? Or is it an avoidable distraction?

This task is important and we hope you may come back to it several times over the course of a week or two, noticing how you are reading at different times, in relation to different kinds of material.

---

**What do you read and why?**

We are surrounded by a sea of print, much of which we read.
We'd like you now to think about what you read, what you like
to read and what you would like to read. Think also about your
reasons for reading different kinds of material. In doing so you
might find the following questions useful:

---

**What do you read and why?**                     *Task 1.6*

What do you read? Magazines? Books? Newspapers? Websites?
Anything in print that comes within striking distance when you
have more than a minute to spare?

Are you addicted to reading? Do you read the backs of cereal
packets; posters at railway stations; those pamphlets about things
that you would rather not imagine, that live in the display racks
in GPs' waiting rooms? Notes on other people's noticeboards?

Can you get on a train or plane, without something to read?

Do you take piles of books on holiday with you? If so, what kind
of books do you take, and why?

Do you get withdrawal symptoms if you don't read a newspaper
for a week?

Are there things you would like to read that you haven't read? If
there are, think about why you would like to read them and try to
work out why you haven't.

Why do you read? Do you have lots of different reasons for reading? Do you ever read without a purpose in mind? Why?

---

At different times your aim in reading may be enjoyment, the
acquisition of information or new viewpoints, passing time, or
some combination of these. Dieters and people who want to reduce their alcohol consumption are often asked to keep a record
of the food they eat or of the alcohol they drink, as a way of
making them more conscious of their eating and drinking. Such
records can be surprising if kept honestly. If you were to keep

a diary of everything you read, you would probably be equally surprised.

---

**Keep a reading diary**            *Task 1.7*

---

Try to keep a diary of everything you read for a week and the amount of time you spend doing so (or perhaps just for a day or two, if a week would be too daunting or time consuming). You will find this quite a major task, because when we say everything, we mean *everything* – from phone books to wine labels, from email messages to the headlines in newspapers, from CD notes to the packets of oven ready meals, and from the abstracts (or even full articles) in academic journals, to websites and academic books.

---

Are you surprised by the amount of time you spend reading each week and by the diversity of the material you read? A reading diary should help you to pinpoint the areas that are your current priorities as a reader, if you didn't already know this.

# PART 2: Reading as a student

In Part 1 we invited you to review your history as a reader. In Part 2 we want to turn to the main event – thinking about yourself as an academic reader, and about the reading you undertake for your course.

## THINKING ABOUT YOUR CAREER AS AN ACADEMIC READER

Whatever reading you have done in the past, and whatever contact you have had with academic books, the reading you are undertaking or will be expected to undertake at university is probably rather different, especially if this is your first contact with higher education. As an undergraduate student you will be directed to some reading by your lecturers – both through 'reading lists' that you are given in relation to particular courses or modules and through references in lectures. However, you will usually have more responsibility for researching and making decisions about what you should read than you had on, for example, your A level or Access course.

In the past most of your academic reading will have been undertaken with textbooks which were specially written for teaching purposes. At university things will be different and you will be required to read a wider range of material. For example, as an undergraduate you will be expected to read at least some books and journal articles in which academics explore new ideas, present new findings and offer arguments in favour of points of view that are contentious and still under debate. You will be expected to demonstrate familiarity with a range of such sources, whenever you write as a student.

You should try, as far as possible, to be aware of the expectations that you bring to your reading and to ensure, if you can, that they are appropriate to the text you are reading. Don't be surprised if you find that articles in journals fail to explain everything in as much detail as you would like. Equally, don't be surprised if a basic encyclopaedic textbook fails to go into every little detail of a topic that you are trying to research. Both types of reading have their place, whatever your level of study. However, generally speaking, as you go through your course you should expect to be reading more specialized material and fewer general texts.

## What and how do you read as a student?

We want to begin our exploration of your career as an academic reader, by asking you to think about what and how you read.

| Thinking about what and how you read | Task 2.1 |
| --- | --- |

What do you read most in connection with your studies? Books? Journal articles?

Is the academic reading you do as a student mostly dictated by your teachers – through required reading, or through references given in the course of lectures?

How much of your academic reading results from following up references you have come across in other things you have read?

Do you ever read academic material out of interest? Or do you only read it because you have to?

Do you ever read academic books from beginning to end? If not, why not?

How many academic books do you read every week? How many do you look at in a week?

Do you ever find your academic reading really interesting – exciting even? Have you ever come across an academic book or article that you 'couldn't put down'? If you have, why do you think this was the case? If you haven't, try to imagine what an academic book that had this effect would be like.

Do you read differently when you are reading in connection with your academic work than when you are reading for enjoyment?

Do you ever find that the reading you have undertaken for an essay doesn't seem to be terribly relevant? Some students do. Sometimes, also, they complain that the reading they are doing doesn't seem relevant to the work they are doing in class. How could this be possible? How could it be that someone spends time in reading material that isn't relevant for them? The answer is simple. If you end up reading stuff that isn't relevant it means that you have not been sufficiently rigorous in selecting what you read. And that means that you are wasting your time.

How much time do you devote to academic reading every week? In thinking about this question, try to take into account not only times when you engage in extensive reading, but also occasions when you look something up in a familiar book, flick through a book to gauge what it is about, or briefly glance through a journal. These are also examples of academic reading; indeed they can sometimes be even more significant than longer reading sessions. A quick glance in a book or article can confirm that it is worth looking at in more detail, while an hour devoted to detailed reading of a book when you are not really in the mood for reading can be a total waste of time.

## Where and when do you do your academic reading?

We want now to get you to think a little about ways in which your reading is influenced by the places in which and the times at which you undertake it. In Part 8 we will continue this discussion, though our focus there will be mainly on offering suggestions about ways in which you might make your reading more effective.

Places can have an effect on the way we feel and not all locations are equally conducive to reading. So, for example, while you might manage to undertake serious reading during a train journey, you might find that buses are never good places to do so. Think carefully about all the places in which you have carried out reading for your course in the last month or so – about whether you read for a long or a short time; about whether you read in a detailed or more cursory way; about whether you were reading material to which you had been directed, or material that you were following up from a reference in something else you read. Think about how you feel when you read in these different places and about how successful you are. Think also about the times at which you do your academic reading. In doing so you might find the following questions helpful.

---

**Where and when do you read as a student?**   *Task 2.2*

Where do you read when you are reading for your academic course? Do you have favourite places?

Where do you find it easiest to read? In the library? In the bath? On the bus? In bed before going to sleep, or after waking in the morning?

Where do you find it hardest to read? How much of your reading do you have to undertake in places where you find it difficult to read? Could you make changes that made it easier to read in these places? Or should you just find somewhere else to read?

Do you find it easy or hard to read in the library? Why?

Are there places that you would find conducive to general reading, but in which you would find academic reading impossible?

When do you find it easiest to read academic material? Why?

Do you undertake your academic reading at particular times of day?

> Are there times of day when you find that, although you can do general reading, serious academic reading would be impossible? Is there anything you could do to make academic reading possible at these times?
>
> Can you do academic reading on holiday?

Some of the difficulties that we experienced while working on this book were caused by incompatibilities between us in terms of the times and locations that suit us best as authors.[6] For example, one of us works best in the morning when the other can barely open his eyes, but can hardly stay awake late at night, never mind following print on a page and making intelligible, far less intelligent, remarks about it. And whereas one of us prefers to get out of the house to do certain joint tasks – in order, for example, to avoid the possibility of interruptions from other family members, the other finds that she can't concentrate on such tasks if she isn't in the house, because she keeps wondering whether everything is OK at home.

Putting in the effort necessary to notice when you are reading successfully will allow you to attempt, so far as possible, to re-create the same conditions when you read in the future. As well as timetabling yourself to read at the best times of day, you will be able to create the optimal physical circumstances in which to do so. Try, for example, always to read in the most helpful place, and to arrange that possible distractions, such as friends and impending hunger or thirst, do not have the chance to intervene between you and your reading goals.

## Why do you read as a student?

Some subjects, especially in the arts and social sciences – such as history, philosophy, literature, sociology and psychology – will involve a lot of reading. Others, notably science and engineering subjects, will usually involve considerably less. The subjects you

---

6 On reflection they seem to be such serious incompatibilities that we can't believe we have managed to put up with one another as academic as well as life partners for so long.

are studying will also affect the kind of reading that you have to undertake. For example, students of literature or theology will have to read many non-academic texts, which in a sense provide the 'raw data' for study; philosophy students will have to read detailed argument, and law students will have to spend time reading reports of legal cases.

In most subjects you will be expected, in your essays and other assignments, to show evidence of reading. You may also be expected to demonstrate familiarity with the literature of your subject in the context of seminars, particularly when you are required to present your work formally. However, individual lecturers will have different expectations about the extent to which you will refer to others in what you say and write, and so it is as well to make sure that you know what they expect.

In his last job one of us was always surprised by colleagues who told students how many references they were expected to use in essays, as if the number of references a person uses offers a gauge of his knowledge about what others have written. If you want to be sure of convincing your lecturers that you really are familiar with what you have read, you should try to make clear, by the way in which you cite others, that you are familiar with what they say. The best way to do this is to be as clear as possible about your reason for citing them. This will probably involve saying something directly about what they believe, argue, demonstrate, or discuss. Consider the following two sentences:

> Research evidence suggests that children learn to read most successfully when both phonic and 'look and say' approaches are adopted (Smith 1991).

> Smith (1991) carried out research which suggests that children are most successful in learning to read, when both phonic and 'look and say' approaches are adopted.

The first of these two sentences gives very little evidence about its author's knowledge of the source cited. We do not know whether Smith carried out the research that is referred to, or merely discusses it; and we are not told anything about the research itself. The second sentence improves upon the first, though the differences between the two are minimal. Even better would be something along these lines:

Smith (1991) carried out a comparative trial with a large sample of schoolchildren across the UK and found that those who were taught to read using both phonic and 'look and say' approaches made significantly faster progress than those who were taught using either approach on its own.

This is a stronger use of the reference to Smith because it demonstrates more knowledge about his research. In Part 7 we say something further about ways in which citation may be used to best effect.

### So why do you read as a student?

The reasons you have for reading are likely to be influenced by the level of study you have reached; they will also be influenced by the subject you are studying and the people who teach you. Some reasons will be personal to you. However, many will be common across students of all subjects and stages, no matter who they are taught by. Some of your reasons for reading will be positive and helpful; some will be less positive and perhaps even detrimental to your development.

---

**Why do students read?**                                   *Task 2.3*

Close this book for a few minutes and 'brainstorm' all the reasons you can think of that you (or other students) might have for reading. Try to do this without looking at the list of reasons that we give below, which is in no particular order. This task could take some time, but it is important.

---

Some of the reasons that we list are reasons that students have shared with us. Some are reasons that students do not immediately recognize. However, when we draw attention to them, students often acknowledge that these reasons do underpin their reading at times. Some reasons that seem superficially similar are actually quite different, because they have a different emotional, intellectual or moral flavour.

## Reasons for reading as a student

To get ideas for essays and assignments.

To expand your knowledge about a subject.

To understand what others have written about topics in which you are interested.

Because lecturers expect to see evidence of reading in essays.

To understand ideas from lectures or seminars, or from other written sources.

To improve your writing style.

To follow up a reference from another source.

Because a particular book, article, chapter, section etc. has been set by a lecturer.

So that you can 'drop names' when you are writing assignments.

So that when you are writing your assignments you can demonstrate familiarity with what others have written.

To contextualize the views you express in your assignments by showing how they relate to what others have said.

Because you are interested in your topic and you want to know more.

To legitimate or back up what you want to say in an assignment.

To give you something to say in your assignments.

Because you've got an exam coming up soon and you'd better learn something or you'll fail.

Because reading what others have said might cause you to change your mind about a subject.

To become a better reader.

Because (like cold showers, vitamin pills and green vegetables) it's good for you.

So that when you come to criticize what others have said, you can do so in an informed way.

For enjoyment.

Because there is a particular piece of information you want or need to find out.

Because you think you ought to read this writer, however boring, because he/she is really important and you should refer to her/him in your essay, or think you should, in order to show that you have read her/him (and anyway, you'll probably get better marks if you do).

Because you paid a lot of money for this set book and want to get your money's worth.

Because your lecturer/tutor wrote the book/article and it might help you understand her views and her research.

Because your lecturer/tutor wrote the book/article, and it's always good to be able to make a reference to something that your lecturer wrote. (If you think this, turn to what we say about taking care in being accurate with all details of references on page 142).

Because the library will only allow this book out on overnight loan, and so it must be important.

## Good and bad, positive and negative reasons for reading as a student

Having thought a little about the different reasons that might underpin reading as a student, we want you now to reflect critically about them.

### Good and bad reasons for reading as a student   *Task 2.4*

Look again at your list and add to it any of the items in our list that you had omitted but which, on reflection, seem important. Now divide it into three separate lists:

i   Reasons that you think are positive and helpful, that is, the reasons that you think are most likely to lead you to reading that is useful because it enhances your learning.

ii   Reasons that you consider negative and unhelpful, that is, reasons that you think are likely to lead to reading that does not enhance your learning.

iii   Reasons that you consider to be neutral, that is, reasons that you do not expect either to lead to or hinder worthwhile work.

One positive reason for reading is that it can stimulate your thinking; another is that reading can help you to improve your writing style, both by learning from the good or even great style in which others write and by allowing you to avoid mistakes made by others. Other positive reasons relate to the wish to contextualize the arguments and points of view that you present in your essays, by relating them to what others have written. They are related to what we consider to be one of the most negative reasons for reading as a student – the intention to 'trophy hunt' for impressive references and apt quotations with which to decorate essays. The point here is that such reading is rarely about getting to grips with what others have said. It is about giving the impression of scholarship, rather than actually being about scholarship.

See page 194 for our complete list of positive and negative reasons for reading as a student.

## Academic readers of different kinds

In Part 1 we invited you to think about the nature of reading and about yourself as a reader and in Part 2 we have begun to focus more specifically on academic reading. In the remainder of the book we will be making suggestions about ways in which you might develop your skills and disciplines as an academic reader. Before doing so, however, we want to ask you to think again about what you are like as an academic reader; we suggest that as you reflect on this, you may wish also to think about the kinds of academic reader that you would like to become.

### *What kind of academic reader are you?*

When we were in the early stages of writing this book our friend Albert Radcliffe, a poet and theologian, set us off on a new line of thought when he shared his idea that, as readers, some people are rather like cloakroom attendants. Such readers collect ideas from lots of different sources, sort them out and organize them on various pegs from which they can be retrieved later. This is an evocative metaphor and thinking about it reminded us of a discussion of different kinds of teacher by Postman and Weingartner in their elderly but still startling book *Teaching as a Subversive Activity* (1977). They talk, for example, about the teacher as a bucket filler (who views his job as being to fill empty minds with knowledge) or as a lamplighter (who views his job as being to illuminate young minds).

Some of Postman and Weingartner's metaphors also lend themselves to a discussion of different kinds of reader – including the reader as a bucket filler, who views reading as a way of filling her mind. Unfortunately bucket filling readers are often rather undiscriminating and are as likely to fill their minds with rubbish as they are to fill them with sparkling gems – worthwhile and well-fashioned ideas.

What are you like as a reader? Are you a bucket filler? Or are you more of an excavator, an archaeologist or a grand prix driver? Perhaps you move between different reading personae, depending on the task in hand?

Excavators dig into what they read with little finesse. They are primarily interested in collecting large amounts of stuff to dump into their essays and are not particularly concerned to ensure that what they dig up is worthwhile – what matters for them is that they give evidence of reading and the more the better. The reader as archaeologist would be appalled. Rather than mechanically digging out what he can from the books and other texts he reads, the reader as archaeologist will dig slowly and carefully, sifting through the rubbish until he finds what he is looking for. Then he will catalogue and label it carefully with other, similar finds, noting down the precise spot where he found it. The reader as archaeologist is interested in gathering evidence to support the theories and arguments he wants to construct, and he will probably compare evidence from several sites in doing so.

The reader as grand prix driver is quite different. He believes in speed. His goal is the end of the chapter, the article, the book or the reading list. He wants to be done with the business of reading as quickly as he can, doesn't have time to collect souvenirs or take snapshots, and in general pays little attention to the intellectual, factual and argumentative scenery he passes through. Some years ago he probably took a speed-reading course and he is very proud of how fast he can travel through text. The grand prix reader notches up books as he passes by, but after a few days can hardly remember their names, never mind what they looked like or the ideas they contained. He will be able to tell you about how much he reads but unless he changes gear quite a lot – when, for example, he comes to difficult sections – he will be able to tell you little about the places he visited in his reading; he may not even know that they exist.

---

**What kind of academic reader are you?**            *Task 2.5*

So what kind of reader are you? Are you more than one, depending on the reading task?

Take some time to reflect about what kinds of reader you are.

Make a list of metaphors for different kinds of reader, with some notes about the characteristics that distinguish each. For example, you may want to think about:

The reader as a juggler (keeping lots of ideas in the air at once).

The reader as a cook (who marinades her own views slowly with snippets of this and that from the sources she reads).

The reader as an explorer (delving deep into unknown and sometimes risky intellectual territory).

The reader as a gardener (who plans carefully, preparing the ground by thinking of questions he wants to ask of the text he is reading; nurturing strong ideas he comes across while weeding out weak specimens).

The reader as a detective (tracking down arguments and lines of thought, both within and between texts).

The reader as a lover (who generously and lovingly massages what she finds into use in writing her assignments).

The reader as map maker (who is involved in sketching out the shape of a book, locating its high points and low points, its interesting features, to allow himself to find his way round during future visits).

---

Each of the metaphors for readers of different kinds we have discussed offers scope for further elaboration, and there are countless others at which we haven't even hinted. Which of them are you? Are you several at different times? How would you classify your friends?

# PART 3: Developing your skills as a reader

In Parts 3 and 4 we discuss our view that being a more success-ful academic reader is more about how you think about reading than it is about developing particular reading skills.

## READ FASTER? READ BETTER?

We want to begin by saying a little about the controversial subject of speed in reading. Some people, convinced by speed-reading gurus, believe that reading faster necessarily means reading better. They are mistaken. Though some people can benefit from read-ing fast some of the time, trying always to read as quickly as possible can lead you to sacrifice understanding for the sake of speed. Woody Allen offers a neat summation of the benefits of speed reading:

> I took a speed reading course, learning to read straight down the middle of the page, and I was able to go through *War and Peace* in twenty minutes. It's about Russia.
> (From *Love and Death*; cited by Williams 1989, p.26)

Our view is that, for most people, the urge to read faster is at best an unhelpful distraction from the business of trying to make one's reading better. Speed in reading has little merit in itself. Nonetheless, students who realize that the work they produce for assignments would become easier and might even get better if they improved their reading often develop the idea that they must learn to read faster. It is as if they think that by reading faster they will be able to read more and that this, in itself, will improve their performance. They are wrong on both counts.

Although they may get through print in a shorter time, those who focus their reading development on the ability to read faster may not actually read more, in the sense of gaining more meaning and information from the words that they process. Although they are jetting through the pages, they may be doing so without touching down to pick up any cargo. Indeed, the whole exercise may begin to seem so pointless that they actually begin to read less.

But let's assume for the moment that speed-reading students do in fact read more, and manage to pick up something from their brief encounter with the words that flash by. Reading more can help you to increase your knowledge and understanding. However, like us, you may have had the experience of reading such a lot about a topic that your head becomes so crammed with new information that it becomes difficult to take in any more, or even to hold on to what you already learned. Worse than that, reading too much can lead to grave problems if you are working for an essay or assignment and time is short (and isn't it always?). For example, having too much information to choose from can make it difficult to select what is relevant and important, especially if you are inclined to believe, as many students are, that everything you read in a book or journal must be important.

We hope you agree with our view that it is never a good use of the time you spend reading to 'cover the ground' without taking some heed of the intellectual scenery through which you are travelling. Even those who promote speed reading would agree with this. The difference between them and us is that whereas they believe that speed reading can benefit most, if not all, readers, provided that they 'keep their eyes peeled', we are sceptical about the usefulness of speed reading for most, though not all, readers.

Barnes (1995) quotes a student who is clearly aware that reading is about picking up intellectual cargo, but seems dissatisfied with the result:

> I'm so busy trying to skim the page as fast as I can that I don't remember anything. I keep thinking 'I've got to hurry ... I must remember this, I must remember that ...' so I don't remember anything in the end.
>
> (Quoted by Barnes 1995, p.50)

Do you identify with this student's experience? If you do, it is time you thought about the best use of your time.

### Make your reading speed fit your purposes

Rather than dashing more and more quickly through more and more written material, it is better to be selective, to read less and to make sure that you understand, retain and make good use of what you read. We are not insisting that all reading must be slow and painstaking, taking in every nuance, every detailed argument. However, you should always make sure that you read at a speed and depth which suits your purposes. You should aim to develop skill in discriminating between times when you require detailed knowledge and understanding – which calls for deliberate, step by step reading of a systematic kind – and times when all that you need is a general idea of what is being said.

If all you need is a general impression of the author's view, you may be able to assess this by skipping quickly through the text, reading odd sections that catch your eye because they contain key words relating to your topic. A number of features of texts make them easy to read in this way, including the markers or signposts that authors use to help readers to find their way around. So, for example, they might punctuate their writing with words and phrases like, 'It follows from this that ...'; 'I want to argue/suggest/point out that ...'; 'Therefore'; 'Thus we can see ...'; 'This leads me to conclude that ...'. In skimming a piece of text to gain a general impression, you may find it helpful to look out for such words and phrases, which can help you to understand what is more and less important. Some authors and some lecturers will be more prescriptive in their advice.

For example, you may come across the suggestion that most paragraphs have a 'topic' sentence which is most often the first sentence, and that, as a result, it is possible to construct a skeleton of any text, by gathering together the key words from the first couple of sentences in each paragraph. Those who offer such advice may list examples of specific signposts that you can expect to find at the beginnings and ends of paragraphs, that give you an indication of their content. For example, they might tell you to look out, at the beginnings of paragraphs, for: 'First of all'; 'To summarize'; 'By contrast'; and 'One important thing to note'. They might go further and suggest that in order to get an impression of an author's view, or to grasp the essence of a chapter, you should read the first and last paragraphs in each chapter (perhaps even the first and last paragraphs of each section), then the first and last sentences in every paragraph. Adopting a strategic approach of this kind to the initial exploration of texts may sometimes produce helpful results. However, you should not expect too much of it. Although some authors give what amounts to an overview of each chapter in both the first 'introductory' paragraph and the final 'concluding' paragraphs, and may even structure their prose in the kind of way that is implied by the idea that all paragraphs contain a 'topic sentence', others will introduce their subject matter more subtly. The best way to read any text will depend both on its subject matter and on the author's style.

## SPEEDING UP YOUR READING

In general we think it is better to read at a pace that allows you to engage with and absorb more of the ideas you are meeting than to read faster while taking in less. We therefore do not intend to attempt to teach you how to read faster. If this is what you want to learn, this book will disappoint you and we suggest that you should consult a book written by those who are committed to the idea that reading faster necessarily means reading better. You should have no difficulty in tracking one of these down, since they are to be found easily enough in most bookshops that cater for academic institutions. However, since slowness in reading is no more a virtue than speed, we want to suggest some steps that should help you to read faster if you find that slowness is causing you problems; they should help you to increase your reading speed without reducing your ability to absorb meaning, and perhaps even enhancing it.

## Thinking about your eyes

As you read, your eyes move across the text. Depending on your level of skill as a reader, the purpose for which you are reading and the type of reading material you are working with, the way in which your eyes do so will differ. For example, you may be reading this page by allowing your eyes to move more or less continuously along each line in turn, lingering over some words and passing over others more quickly. More likely, however, you will move your eyes in a series of steps from left to right across each line, until the end of the line is reached, when they will move to the beginning of the next line, following it to the end and so on, until you reach the end of the page. In other words, your eyes may be moving in this kind of way.

For example, you may be reading this page by allowing

your eyes to move more or less continuously along each line

in turn, lingering over some words and passing over others

fairly rapidly. More likely, however, you will move your

eyes in a series of steps from left to right across each line,

until the end of the line is reached.

The number of steps you take to move across each line will depend, for example, on how good a reader you are, and the type of material you are reading. Some readers will fix on each word. For such a reader the first sentence of this paragraph would go a little like this:

The – number – of – steps – you – take – to – move – across – each – line – will – depend – for – example – on – how – good – a – reader – you – are – and – the – type – of – material – you – are – reading.

Anyone who habitually reads like this will have some difficulties, because it takes attention away from the overall sense of the sentence. Reading each word individually as – if your – life – depended – on – it, or even reading the individual syllables of the bigger words sep–ar–ate–ly, which some people undoubtedly do, especially when they come across words with which they are unfamiliar, can make it difficult to understand what an author is saying.

More sophisticated readers tend to fix less often.[7] In this case the sentence above would go a little like this:

The number of steps – you take – to move across each line – will depend – for example – on how good a reader you are – and the type of material – you are reading.

It is easy to see how someone who reads like this, taking in longer chunks of meaningful text at a time, will be able to understand what he is reading more easily than one who is limited to reading word for word.

The methodical movement across the page from left to right and from top to bottom that these examples illustrate is what most of us associate with reading. It mirrors the linear way in which our language works. Words follow one another in long streams and make sense by being understood in accordance with the accepted principles of grammar and conventions of punctuation that we understand when we are reading, even if, as writers, we are less sure of them. As we become more used to the ways in which texts work, and develop higher order skills, we begin to approach reading in a range of different ways, depending on our

---

7 A good way of helping yourself to speed up your reading by fixing less frequently is to use a guide when you are reading. Try moving a pencil or a finger smoothly under each line as you read it. Don't be put off by the fact that you may remember doing something similar as a child, since this tactic can actually increase your reading speed by getting you to move your eyes faster across the page. Try it.

purposes. As a result, there is a change in the ways in which our eyes move across text.

Think for a moment about how your eyes move when you are trying to locate particular words or ideas in a piece of text. Then turn to pages 111–12 and look for the words 'fetus' and 'baby'; turn to pages 122–3 and look for anything that is said about 'ethics' or 'morality'. How did your eyes move? Did they start at the top of the page and move over each line in turn? Did they move down the middle of the page, stopping at two or three places where they scanned chunks of text on either side? Or did they scan the page in a seemingly random way?

| **How do you read for information?** | *Task 3.1* |
| --- | --- |

Leave this book for a while and find another one – preferably one with which you are unfamiliar. Try reading a few pages (any few pages) well enough to allow you to give an account of their main ideas. Then, when you read on, try to be conscious of the ways in which your eyes are moving.

How did you get on? Did it take you more or less time than you would have anticipated to grasp the main ideas? Did you find your eyes moving word by word across the page, fixing on each in turn? Or did you find them jumping across each line in a series of leaps, like a bouncing ball? If you did, was there some rationale to where they fixed? For example, did they fix on difficult or key words? Or did they fix at regular intervals as they passed across the page – at a rate of, say, three fixes a line? Did you find yourself subvocalizing at all – i.e. pronouncing words under your breath? If so, did this happen with each word? Or did it only happen when you came to longer and more difficult words, or words with which you are unfamiliar? Incidentally, how have you been reading this paragraph? Have you been stopping at the end of each question, trying to work out the answer?

## Guessing ahead, key words and meaningful chunks of text

When you were reading from another book for the last task you probably used a number of fairly advanced reading techniques, including making use of what you already know, to guess ahead at what is to come, spotting the most important, or key, words, and reading whole chunks of text at a time.

### Guessing ahead

A large part of reading is guesswork or anticipation. As we read we use the meanings we pick up to guess ahead at what is to come; that way we are able to move more quickly through text. You are probably well aware of this, but if you aren't, try reading a page or two of unfamiliar text using a marker which you place below each line. At the end of each line hazard a guess at what comes next and see how often your guess makes sense. This is a good way of getting children who are just beginning to read to focus on the fact that reading is about getting meanings from the text, and of teaching them to guess ahead, actively making meaning as they read. It is also, incidentally, a good way of slowing yourself down, or of forcing yourself to attend to the meaning of texts if you are reading when you are tired, or if you feel bored by what you are reading.

### Key words and meaningful chunks of text

Following on from what we have said about the ways in which your eyes move across the page when you are reading, one simple way in which you can probably increase your reading speed would be to cut down the number of times your eyes fix in moving across each line. For example, if you are in the habit of fixing on every word, you might try to make it every other word or every third or fourth word; or perhaps two times a line or only on significant words; or you might try to focus on key words – those that carry most of the meaning. Consider the sentence:

One of the principal aims of the study was to develop guidelines for good practice for the School of Care Sciences at the University of Glamorgan.

The key words in this sentence seem to be:

> principal aims – study – develop guidelines – good practice
> – School – Care Sciences – University – Glamorgan.

You may disagree with our view of the key words. For example, you may think that 'One' is a key word, because it alerts us to the fact that the aim described is only one among a number of important aims in this study.

If you read for key words, you will find that very often they cluster together with a few other words, in meaningful chunks of text. Our knowledge of the ways in which words of different kinds function allows us to group words together, reading whole chunks of text rather than individual words, and this can help us to read faster and with more understanding. So, for example, we know that in the phrase 'big red balloon', 'big' and 'red' are adjectives which elaborate or describe a noun, in this case 'balloon'; that is why we are more likely to read 'big red balloon' than 'big – red – balloon'. And in the example above, 'principal aims'; 'develop guidelines'; 'for good practice', or even 'develop guidelines for good practice', obviously cluster together in meaningful chunks and are important to the sense that the person who wrote them is attempting to convey.

However, words also cluster together in meaningful chunks when they are inessential to the sense that authors are trying to convey. On pages 56–7 we discussed a paragraph from a student essay, which contains several meaningful chunks that nonetheless add little to the student's intended sense. Consider, for example, the sentence which begins, 'The literacy hour as it is currently set up has a number of different parts', in which the phrase 'as it is currently set up' is meaningful, but adds nothing, even though something might have been added by telling something about the ways in which the literacy hour is currently set up. Readers who can take in and assess whole chunks of text will usually find it easier to skip by sections that are marginal or even irrelevant to the topic under discussion. They will thus manage both to read faster and to extract more meaning from texts than those who are compelled, whether by lack of practice, habit or skill, to fix on every individual word.

**Reading for key words**            **Task 3.2**

Look at the following sentences and identify the words that, for you, are key words – that is, words that you would fix on as you read.

i The hardness of wood is caused basically by lignin and cellulose thickening the cell walls, the degree of hardness depending on the amount of lignification and the percentage of thick-walled fibers present.
(Bold, H.C. *The Plant Kingdom*, 1964, p.52)

ii The whole unnumbered tribe of wooing and plighted lovers were for him unconscious actors in a world-comedy of Love's contriving – naïve fools of fancy, passionately weaving the cords that are to strangle passion.
(C.H. Herford, in J. McFarlane, *Henrik Ibsen: A Critical Anthology*, 1970, p.81)

iii Thus the principles of paternalism are those that the parties would acknowledge in the original position to protect themselves against the weakness and infirmities of their reason and will in society.
(Rawls, J. *A Theory of Justice*, 1973, p.249)

iv Forced into retirement at his country cottage, Machiavelli gambled with the local boors at the village inn, returning home each evening to don his best clothes, enter his study and hold intellectual converse with the great authors of classical Antiquity.
(Dickens, A.G. *The Age of Humanism and Reformation*, 1977, p.99)

v Gender stereotypes indicate that in conversation adult men are more likely to assert, challenge, make statements or ignore than are women, while women tend to use conversation constructively to negotiate or maintain relationships.
(R. Hinde, in D. Miell and R. Dallos (eds) *Social Interaction and Personal Relationships*, 1996, p.325)

How did you get on? The words that we considered to be key words are to be found on page 196. Notice the overlap between this task and what we say about key wording as an approach to note taking, which we discuss at some length in Part 6, and in which key words often play a significant role.

---

**Practise reading for key words**                                    *Task 3.3*

Even though it may feel peculiar to do so, you may find it useful to practise reading unfamiliar passages, trying as far as possible to fix only on key words, dancing lightly by less significant ones.

Leave this book for a while and find a couple of others:
- one that relates to work you are doing for your course
- one that does not relate to your course

Read a few pages of each book while making the conscious attempt to fix only on key words. After you have finished reading make a few notes about the main points in the pages you have read in each book, but do so with the book closed.

---

How did you get on? Did you find that looking for and focusing on key words speeded up, or slowed down, your reading? How often did the key words on which you fixed appear in your notes? Did you find it easier or harder to read for key words when you were reading about your subject area?

---

**Reading for key words as a way of removing**          *Task 3.4*
**what's unimportant in your written work**

In Part 10 we talk about the importance of learning to read your own work critically. Skill in reading for key words can be a great help in spotting what is essential and what inessential in what you write.

Read the following extract from a student essay, for key words. List the key words as you see them (our list appears on page 197).

It would seem that the most important single feature of the literacy hour in our primary schools is the fact that it involves all of the children in the class working together with the teacher in a group. The literacy hour as it is currently set up has a number of different parts which focus on texts at a number of different levels like the word level which relates to single words and the text level which is the level of the book as a whole. Although when it was first set up many teachers did not like the literacy hour, because it got in the way of all their other important work of various kinds with the children in their classes, it is now well accepted. Ultimately it would seem that through the many and varied activities that form part of the literacy hour as a whole, the children begin to work as a group which can only be a good thing in the end.

We have chosen a passage from rather a poor essay, because it is useful in illustrating how reading for key words can help you to spot what is inessential in a passage. It is full of redundant or almost redundant words and phrases which add little or nothing to the meaning.[8] For example, in the last sentence we find, 'Ultimately it would seem that', 'many and varied', 'as a whole' and 'which can only be a good thing in the end', none of which adds very much to the sense of the sentence. You may disagree with this assessment. In particular you may argue that the words 'it would seem that' convey the sense that the author is rather tentative and of course, it could do this. However, the fact that a couple of sentences earlier the same phrase was also used leads us to suspect that it has not been used – knowingly – for this purpose, but is, rather, an unhelpful stylistic 'tic' or mannerism in this student's writing. In Part 10, when we come to talk about different ways of reading your own work, we say something about the importance of becoming aware of such mannerisms and removing them.

---

8 Some words are grammatically important but inessential in conveying the intended meaning; others are redundant because they are neither important in conveying meaning nor in supporting the passage as a piece of grammatically correct English.

| Try reading some of your own work for key words | Task 3.5 |
|---|---|

In Part 10, we discuss the importance of learning to read your own work as if you did not write it. Though we do not want to pre-empt that discussion, we want you now to try reading a piece of your own work for key words.

Did you find it easy? Did you find lots of words that were not key words, or only a few? Did reading for key words help you to spot redundant words and phrases? Did you spot any stylistic 'tics' and mannerisms?

## Skimming, scanning and sampling

Most books about study skills include discussions of reading techniques, which overlap with some of what we have talked about in Part 3 so far. They are referred to using a variety of names, including 'skimming', 'skipping', 'scanning', 'sampling' and so on, though there is a great deal of variability in the ways in which these terms are used. We do not intend to enter into a detailed discussion of the differences between these approaches. However, we do want to say something about their usefulness as a way of gathering information from texts.

*Skimming* is often proposed as a useful way of getting a general sense of what a text is about. Our guess is that, like most people, you probably skim quite a lot of the time, both when you are reading in connection with your course and, for example, when you are reading magazines and newspapers.

In books that aim to teach study skills, you might find skimming described in a number of ways, which belong to a family of approaches:

- Allowing your eyes to pass down the middle of the page taking in important words on either side. This involves gambling that the omission of words from the edges of the page is not too significant and that you will be able to guess at their meaning from what you do take in.

idea about what it is about; this, in turn, will help you to decide how to go about tackling it in detail. Skimming will help you to find such sections, as will the discipline of scanning for key concepts that you have located using the index and contents list. Combining skimming and scanning in this way can thus help you to avoid getting bogged down in difficult text.

Skimming can also help you to decide what kind of text you are dealing with – for example, whether it contains information or description or argument. It can be a good way of getting the gist of what is said and of gauging whether the level of information presented is sufficient for your needs. However, it cannot help you to extract meaning at a deeper level. For that you will have to read in a detailed way, thinking and asking questions as you go, allowing yourself the opportunity to think about what is said, taking the time to absorb information and to reflect on the strength of arguments. Reading of this kind must be active and in Part 4 we discuss active reading in some detail.

---

| **Circuit training for reading** | *Task 3.6* |
|---|---|

Whatever approaches you habitually adopt in your reading, you will find it worthwhile, every so often, to take the time to engage in a bit of 'circuit training' aimed at developing stamina and strength as a reader. Set yourself some small tasks, similar to the one you have just carried out. In each case, give yourself a prescribed time to accomplish the task, preferably a bit less time than you estimate it would take to do a thorough job. For example,

  i   Give yourself a short time (perhaps 15–30 minutes) to write some notes about the main points in a chapter or article that you want to read.

  ii  Give yourself one hour to write brief notes on six journal articles.

  iii Pick out the main points in an argument contained in a longer piece of text (a book or article, say) and rearrange them in a form that is easier to understand, then commit them to memory. (Depending on the length and complexity of the argument and the clarity with which the author has presented it, you might expect this to take anything from five minutes to half an hour.)

iv Write a brief overview of a book that is new to you, but which you really want to get to know; your overview should remind you of the main points and the main locations in which you will find them. Take no more than an hour.

v Set yourself a topic about which you would like to write an essay, and take one hour to find three books (or three articles) in the library that will help you to find out about it; note down key words and pages where you can find them.

vi Give yourself a short time to reread an essay that you have written, noting down key words, and prepare a three-minute presentation about your views for someone who knows nothing at all about this area (you might even want to try it on a friend). Make sure you stick to the key points.

## VISITING A BOOK FOR THE FIRST TIME

In discussing the range of different ways in which it is possible to approach a new book, Marshall and Rowland (1993) coin a powerful metaphor, likening a visit to a new book to a visit to a new city.

There are many ways in which we might visit new places. For example, many years ago, one of us stopped in Amsterdam for a few hours with a coachload of students. It was his first visit and he decided to spend his time in doing two things, apart from having something to eat. First, he visited the Rijksmuseum, a famous art gallery, and then he wandered aimlessly round the narrow streets and canals, soaking up the atmosphere.

Had he been visiting a new book he might have done similar things. For example, if he was following up a detailed reference, he would be able to go immediately to the appropriate part of the book, just as his visit to the Rijksmuseum was inspired by the knowledge that it contained paintings that he wanted to examine at first hand. On the other hand, if his information was less detailed, for example if he was following up a number of vague references to it, he would probably first of all browse in an exploratory way. This would be similar to the second, wandering, part of his visit to Amsterdam. Incidentally, the fact that during this part of his visit he happened upon a famous commercial area which caused him to blush, despite the fact that he was well aware of its existence beforehand,[9] reinforces the idea that even when one is merely wandering about a new city taking in the atmosphere, it might be as well to give some thought to the areas in which one wishes to wander. The same thing is also true of visits to new books which may not cause you to blush but may nonetheless cause you some discomfort.

Of course there are other ways to visit a new city, including having a detailed list of places – galleries, buildings, shops, parks, red light districts and so on – that one wishes to visit. Similarly, when following up specific references, one will have a list of locations in a new book, which address particular topics in which one is interested. And just as, following an initial brief exploration to get our bearings, we might set about exploring a city's treasures in a systematic way, we will often approach a book that we have already assessed as being worthy of systematic reading in a careful, painstaking and methodical way.

Whenever you are deciding to read a new book, you should decide what kind of visit you want to pay to it. Are you going there as a kind of intellectual tourist on a day trip, checking out what is worth going back to look at in more detail? Or do you already have particular places that you want to visit for specific purposes? (In which case you may want to plan the best order for your various visits, in the same way as you might plan a tour round the places you want to visit in a new city.)

| | |
|---|---|
| **Skimming, scanning and sampling: books and cities** | *Task 3.7* |

It occurs to us that there is a two-way metaphor here. Just as the idea of visiting a city as a tourist can be metaphorically applied to visiting a new book, so ideas about reading – for example about different ways of reading, including scanning, skimming and sampling – might be used to think about ways of visiting a new city. Can you see why?

---

9 If you don't understand why he blushed, you may want to ask a more worldly-wise friend about why certain areas of this charming city might have this effect.

# PART 4: Active reading: developing a relationship with texts and their authors

In Part 3 we focused on the idea of improving your reading by developing specific reading skills. In Part 4 we invite you to think about different approaches to academic reading and suggest some steps that will help you to make sure that your reading is as beneficial as it might be.

## DON'T BE A PASSIVE READER AND DON'T TAKE WHAT YOU READ AT FACE VALUE

Many students believe, or act as if they believe, that while authors have something to say and knowledge to share, the job of the reader is merely to access and assimilate such knowledge. We want to challenge this belief, which views reading as passive and uncritical and the reader merely as a sponge, soaking up ideas and information. It underpins the unhealthy tendency uncritically to view academic authors as authorities, which we discuss below. Of course, some authors are authorities in the sense that they have demonstrated knowledge and expertise to such an extent that others within their field generally recognize them as having

something worthwhile to say. However, they are usually authorities in relation to a strictly limited area – probably one in which
they have research interests or professional expertise.

A more healthy way to view academic authors and the things
they write is to see them as participants in a public exchange of
views, whose contributions need to be evaluated against criteria
such as relevance, coherence, clarity and strength of argument.

## Over-reliance on the authority and reliability of academic texts

You will have to develop the ability to discriminate between
situations in which authors are presenting knowledge, or something that is commonly taken to be knowledge, and situations in
which they are presenting their own ideas, observations, results
and arguments.[10] Since a wide variety of views are to be found
about most topics, you will also have to develop skill in critically
assessing the views that authors present and the evidence and
arguments that they use in presenting those views. This skill will
allow you to decide which views to embrace and which views
could be useful in developing your own ideas.

In building your own arguments or points of view, there are
many ways in which you can make use of your reading and we
discuss some of these in Part 7. Too many students limit themselves to using authors who agree with their views, to 'back up'
what they are saying – as if they cannot refer to views they
disagree with, or believe to be flawed. Reliance on the authority
of academic authors and their publications is at least partly responsible for the tendency among some, and perhaps many, students to act as if they do not believe that they have anything to

---

10 It is also as well to bear in mind that, from time to time, ideas and beliefs that
were once accepted as knowledge are shown to be false, and relegated to a
great catalogue of ideas that are now thought to fall short of knowledge.
Consider, for example, the fact that the world used to be flat and is now
round, and that until less than a century ago atoms were thought to be the
smallest objects in the universe, whereas they are now known to be truly
cosmic in proportion, when compared to the current front runners for the
smallest things in the world – the so-called 'strings' that are thought to be at
the heart of everything.

say themselves, and to devalue their own ability to think. Sometimes this can convey an impression of laziness, even though it may arise from simple uncertainty, both about their ability and about what is expected of them.

Students who fall into the trap of believing that being in print necessarily conveys authority often treat the authors of books, articles, CD ROMs and Internet websites as if they possess and speak the truth, even when what they are saying is poorly stated, poorly argued and poorly supported by evidence. The better known the authors, the more likely it is that what they write will be uncritically accepted by such students. We wish we had a pound for every student we have ever known who has cited an author as if doing so necessarily strengthened his own point of view, without any apparent attempt to assess what that author had to say. (Actually we wish we had a pound for every academic article we have read in which the author has done the same thing.)

Students who approach academic reading in this naïve way sometimes seem to believe that the answers to the questions they are set as part of their course are to be found virtually ready made, in the things they read. That is why they often ask their lecturers what they 'need to read' for each essay or assignment, as if it is only in certain sources that answers are to be found, and as if the task is to locate those answers and regurgitate them, or perhaps, given awareness of the serious view that is taken of plagiarizing, to paraphrase them.[11] It is also why some students feel frozen into inaction if they discover that a book they have decided they need for their work (or that their lecturer – most often unwisely in our view, has told them they should read) is unavailable. We hope that you do not recognize yourself in this description, which has some overlap with the activity that we refer to, for obvious reasons, as 'the search for the Holy Grail', one of a large number of techniques employed by those (including

---

11  Paraphrasing another person's views is acceptable and can be useful as a way of showing that one understands what they have said or written. Unfortunately, some students develop the habit of paraphrasing authors without acknowledging that they are doing so. This is plagiarism just as much as if they had stolen the author's words. It involves either the deceitful dodge of adopting as their own, ideas that belong to someone else, or sloppy note-taking habits.

professional academics as well as students) who want to avoid getting down to work.

The 'Holy Grail', which figures in the legend of King Arthur, was the mythical vessel used by Christ during the last supper, celebrated in the Christian sacrament of holy communion. To 'search for the Holy Grail' is to seek for an unfindable (or probably unfindable) treasure. It involves becoming so hooked on the idea that a particular text holds the answer to all your questions that you believe, or act as if you believe, that you can't do anything until it has been found. Usually the Grail is a book or source that you cannot seem to pin down; for example, it may only be available on overnight loan and you might discover that there is an impossibly long waiting list; or it may only be possible to obtain it on inter-library loan from some little known college in Indiana. People rarely find their Holy Grail, which is usually an individual thing – what is the Grail for you would not be the Grail for us, for example. What's more, if they do find it, the Holy Grail often turns out to be nothing but a mirage – something that looked inviting, but had no substance – at which point another text usually takes on the mantle of the Holy Grail.

In addition to relying too much on particular texts as the primary source of material for their essays and assignments, and devaluing their own thinking, students who do not develop critical skills as readers may rely too much on the use of quotation. It is almost as if they do not have sufficient trust in their ability to understand what authors are saying to believe that they can give a reliable account, in their own words, of the ideas a book or article contains. In extreme cases this can lead to essays and assignments which look rather like patchwork quilts, made up of quotations from others which have been joined loosely together in a way that demonstrates little more than the student's ability to copy down and rearrange words that others have written. It can lead to the impression that those who produce such pseudo-essays have acted more like editors than authors.

Lest you should feel offended at the idea that we might consider you lazy if you are in the habit of quoting rather a lot, ask yourself what takes more effort – quoting an author's words directly, or trying to understand and engage with her. Quoting another person takes less time and frees you to do other things, but in most circumstances it is unlikely to help you to carry out good academic work. Of course, in some subjects, such as literature, the liberal use of quotation is expected. However, in a sense the inclusion of sections of text in such subjects is analagous to the presentation of data in science and hence different from the quotation of parts of intellectual positions or arguments that we are talking about.

The view of academic reading that we are rejecting is closely related to an unhelpful way of thinking about teaching and learning in which students are viewed as buckets which teachers are thought to be responsible for filling with ideas and information (see page 44). Unfortunately this view is fairly common; many students look to their lecturers principally as sources of knowledge. It is even present among some of those lecturers, in spite of the fact that as a view of teaching and learning it is even less appropriate at university than it is during the school years.

Students who embrace the bucket model of academic reading usually have a limited relationship with the texts they read. This will probably show in their writing. When they visit books and articles, they are likely simply to harvest ideas, information and nice sounding quotations with which to fill their assignments, rather than allowing the texts they read to bring about lasting changes in the ways they think, or in the things they know. They may waste much of their reading time in trying, indiscriminately, to memorize what they read. Even if the ideas and facts that a student commits to memory in this unthinking way are useful for his purposes (and much of the time they won't be), learning of this kind is likely to be less useful than learning that relates what is learned to what is already known and understood. Not only that, but unless he does something actively to relate what he reads about to the knowledge he already possesses, thus in a sense making it his own, a student is unlikely to retain more than a very small proportion of it. The best learning is always tied into the body of knowledge the student already possesses.

## APPROACHING ACADEMIC READING

The most important thing in your development as a reader is that you should find ways of reading that suit you. This will include making choices about where and when to read for different purposes; what kinds of material to read, and how much to read; whether you should always read on your own, or whether you should sometimes share your reading with friends. You will also have to decide on the best strategies to adopt in reading different kinds of texts. Such choices will depend upon a number of factors including:

- the stage that your relationship with the text has reached – whether, for example, you are good friends, or have just met in a corner of a library or bookshop
- the time you have available – whether you have time to savour the time you spend together, or rather (like illicit lovers) you have to snatch odd moments together
- your reasons for reading – for example, whether you are assessing the text for relevance, are looking for particular information, or are studying it as a set part of your course.

### How do you read newspapers and magazines?

Do you start at the beginning and read your way through till you get to the end? Probably not. When they pick up a newspaper or magazine, most people know pretty much what they are interested in reading and, what's more, they know how to find it. This is true even of relatively uneducated people. For example, when one of us asked a friend, who left school at 14 and claims only ever to have read two books, how he reads newspapers, he replied:

Well generally I look at the headlines and any pictures to see if anything interesting's happened, then I turn to the back pages for the sport and after that I go inside where there's the letters page and the crossword.

His strategy for reading magazines is similar but involves using the contents list to decide what articles and features are worth looking at.

David's approach to reading newspapers and magazines is similar to the way our daughter assesses books she is thinking of reading, which we discussed on page 27. How does it compare with:

- the ways in which you asssess whether an academic book or article is worth reading?
- the ways you read a newspaper or magazine?

Your approach to reading newspapers and magazines is probably fairly similar to David's. Whether they are interested in serious political commentary, fashion or sport, most people usually know where to turn to in their regular newspaper or in any newspaper they pick up. In the case of magazines they will probably, like David, be able to use the contents page (which may be detailed enough to double as a kind of index) and the brief summaries which appear at the beginning of some magazines (which are similar to the abstracts of articles in academic journals) to locate articles that may interest them. They certainly won't waste time in reading newspaper and magazine articles from beginning to end, 'just in case' they turn out to be interesting. How odd, then, that so many students try to read academic texts from beginning to end, blindly hoping that something of interest will turn up.

### Developing a strategic approach to reading

Naturally we are most concerned, not with the ways in which you read newspapers and magazines, but with the way you read academic texts, including books and journal articles. The way you approach such texts should vary according to your purposes, and to make the best possible use of your reading you should try to be as clear as you can about what you are aiming to achieve.

How often do you find yourself several pages or even chapters into a book you believe to be important for your academic work, only to come to your senses half an hour or even an hour later, realizing that you have little idea what you have been reading about? This common experience results from the tendency to fall headlong into a piece of text without noticing that you are doing so, allowing yourself to be carried along in a swirl of language taking you nowhere as words flow in front of your eyes but fail to engage with your brain. It happens to us all but we can avoid it. Indeed, if you want to be as efficient as you can be as a student you will have to learn to avoid it, because it involves squandering time and effort.

### Sorting out your reasons for reading

Before you even open a book or look at the first page of a photocopied article, make sure that you are aware of your reasons for doing so. Always ask yourself what you hope or expect to gain from reading before you begin working on a new text. This will allow you to make sensible decisions about how to approach it – about whether, for example, you should read in detail or more quickly, and whether you should take notes, or mark the text in some way – for example, by underlining or highlighting key words and/or annotating the text with your own comments and questions.[12]

For example, are you reading in order to understand a particular argument or point of view? Or do you want to skim the text quickly in order to gauge its relevance and locate sections that will repay methodical reading? Are you searching for a particular view or idea, or piece of information that you need in order to undertake an assignment? Are there specific questions to which you want to find answers?

Bearing in mind your purpose as you read will help you to remain alert and to make good use of your reading. As you read, try every so often to review your understanding of the text. You can either do this by recalling what you have read, in your mind, or by writing (without reference to the text) some notes about it. Frequently stopping in this way can help you to avoid a situation where you find your mind overflowing with so many ideas and arguments that you have not really thought about properly, that you cannot remember them all clearly, compelling you to reread. When you are reading slowly and methodically, it might be good to develop the habit, at the end of each page, of asking yourself the extent to which this page has helped you to fulfil the

---

12 What do you think about writing in books? Does it shock you that we have even raised the possibility? (It does shock some people.) Or does it seem like a natural thing to do? We both write in books at times, and sometimes rather a lot, because we find that it helps us to read more efficiently. We say more about this in Part 6, when we discuss note taking.

task you have set yourself, or to answer the questions you are asking. However, you should beware of the possibility that doing so might lead you to 'lose the thread' a little and so you should not follow this advice unless you already have a decent grasp of the overall picture. In general it is best always to read a text more than once, and only ever to undertake detailed reading after an initial exploratory reading.

Another way of avoiding the experience we have been discussing, in which a failure in concentration results in words and ideas seeming to float before your eyes while bypassing your brain, is to develop the habit of taking notes as you read. However, this is only to be recommended when you have decided, on the basis of an initial overview, that a piece of text is worth reading in detail and there are particular questions to which you want to find answers. We discuss the process of taking notes in Part 6. For the moment we want to draw your attention to the danger that, unless you remain aware of what you wish to take notes about, you might do so on automatic pilot, so that you do not recognize them when you finally wake up. Indeed, depending on the approach to note taking you adopt, the process of taking notes might even increase the chances that your reading will become unfocused. For example, it could do this if (like some students) your approach is to act rather like a distorting photocopier, rendering text into 'your own words', in a fairly indiscriminate way, without making the attempt to comprehend it, far less to engage critically with it. In such circumstances you may get to the end of a passage, and discover that a version of the text you have read seems to have passed from your eye to the pen in your hand and out onto the page, without passing anywhere near your brain.

Have you ever had this experience – of taking notes while reading, only to discover after an hour or so that, although you have written several pages, you really have no idea at all what they mean? It is rather like the experience of driving on a motorway and being so caught up in the immediate task of negotiating your way among the hordes of other drivers and vehicles that, half an hour later, when you realize that you are nearing the exit you want, you can't remember how you got there. Readers with physiological knowledge will no doubt assure us that there are no neural pathways from eye to hand via the shoulder, that avoid the brain. Actually we knew this already. Nonetheless, accuracy in describing the physiological basis of the phenomenon we are describing, in which notes seem to appear on the page without the person who wrote them having thought about what they mean, is less important to us than the fact that it does occur and is to be avoided.

### Sorting out your purposes and expectations

Always try to be clear about your purposes as a reader and beware of placing expectations on yourself that are unhelpful or stressful, or unlikely to help you achieve your aim of reading as well and as efficiently as possible. Consider, for example, the idea of going to the library to read for a set period of time, which some students sometimes see as a good thing in itself. (Do you ever do this? And if you do, do you usually know pretty much what you are hoping to achieve?) At a superficial level, an hour of reading seems like a positive thing to do and it can be, provided that you have a good reason for doing so. However, reading mindlessly for 60 long minutes in order to be able to notch up an hour against some set amount that you imagine you have to achieve is a bad use of time. Strange though it may seem, many students (you may be one of them) will in any case find it best to avoid reading in the library because of the temptation – all too common in university libraries – of grasping at the first opportunity to stop reading, for example when a friend or acquaintance – or even someone you cannot stand – suggests going for a 'quick' coffee. 'After all,' the classic, self-deceiving excuse goes, 'there isn't much point in reading when I don't seem to be getting anywhere. Better to have a rest and come back refreshed, after a break.' Unless you are a highly unusual character, you are familiar with this tactic for avoiding work. We certainly are – both when it is used by others and when we use it ourselves.

Reading for the sake of reading has no value whatever. Unless it is combined with a thoughtful choice of predetermined reading task, or a particularly wise (or fortuitous) choice of reading material, going to the library or locking yourself in your room with no aim other than reading for a predetermined time is likely to lead to boredom, so that you end up mindlessly staring at text, without engaging your brain, in the kind of way we have referred to above. On the other hand, setting yourself a particular period in which to accomplish a reading task which you set yourself can be helpful as a way of getting yourself to focus. You may, for example, want to try giving yourself a certain time to read a particular article, chapter, section or passage. The more focused the task the better. For instance, it could be positive to set yourself a particular period of time in which to assess the relevance, for your purposes, of a number of books or articles; to understand an important but difficult argument; or to locate material in and take notes about a source that you have good reason to believe can help you to answer a particular question. If you try this tactic to help you focus as a reader, don't be despondent if, as may well happen, you get so absorbed that you overrun the time you have set yourself. This could well be a positive thing, especially if you have been avoiding this particular piece of reading for a while.

Sometimes the difficulty with reading, as with many other jobs, is simply how to get started. One way round this problem when you encounter it is to set yourself really small and manageable reading tasks. For example, when you are finding difficulty getting started with a book, you might decide to begin by finding three interesting sections in the contents list, to note four key words from the index or to read the abstract or the first page. The task should be one that is useful towards your final aim of getting your essay or paper or dissertation written, or revising for your exam, but small enough for it to be hardly conceivable that you could not complete it however tired, depressed, lonely or bored you are. In devising such tiny but 'do-able' tasks for yourself you are using your creativity, making the reading a personal task to you and breaking a large endeavour up into small and attainable steps. You may have heard the phrase 'You don't have to be great to get started, but you have to get started to be great.' The next day or the next time you come to this piece of reading, the work of making a beginning will have been done and you will already have achieved something with this text and so the next stage should follow more easily.

Often the motivation supplied by an assignment or essay will help you to focus your reading in helpful ways. When you are reading at other times – for example, in an attempt to expand on ideas and information that you have picked up in lectures or seminars – inventing possible essay topics for yourself will often be a good way of structuring your reading. Try it now.

| Reading round a topic | Task 4.1 |
| --- | --- |

Set yourself an essay topic – it can be on anything at all to do with your course. Then visit your university or college library and find six books or articles that would help you to write about this topic.

For each book or article, write a full and accurate reference. If you have any doubts about how to write references, see Part 7, where we offer examples of the Harvard system of referencing.

Following the reference to each book or article, write a paragraph or two in which you outline the main points of the text that are relevant to the task you have set yourself. Then write a list of key words to give yourself a quick guide to remembering what the article contains.

Finally, compile an alphabetical reference list in which you give details for each of the books or articles you have studied.

One way of thinking about the work you are doing on these texts is to think of yourself as developing extended references in relation to them.

## ACTIVE READING: DEVELOPING AS A DISCIPLINED READER

In order to make the best possible use of the time you spend reading, it is important that you learn to read actively, engaging with the meanings that authors are attempting to communicate. Rather than merely following the words on the page with your eyes, perhaps hearing them sound in your head as you do so, you need consciously to make the effort to understand them – and to notice when you are failing to do so. Whenever we offer this advice to students, we do so rather self-consciously, because it seems like such an obvious thing to say. After all, once we get past the stage of 'barking at print',[13] we are surely aware that reading is about meaning.

Yet most people will confess to 'reading', at times, with little awareness of what they are reading about. And so we do not really want to inform you that to make good use of the time you spend reading, you must read with understanding, because you knew as much before you began reading this book. Rather we want to draw your attention to the need to keep reminding yourself to read in such a way that you are actively pursuing meaning and understanding.

## Make meaning as you read

If your reading is to be as useful as it might be, it will have to be not only about the attempt to take meaning from texts, by absorbing the information and points of view they present, but about making meaning in relation to them. Active reading involves the attempt to establish connections between the meanings that the author is trying to convey and what you already know. Making the attempt to bring all of your previous knowledge and experience to bear when you read:

- can help you to understand the author
- can help you to remember what the author is communicating
- may kindle your creativity and produce interesting (and perhaps even original) thoughts, as the ideas and facts and arguments that you are reading about collide with those you are already carrying around in your head.

We tend both to understand and remember things best when we can relate them to what we already know, when we can knit them together into a complex web of interconnections. One of

---

13 This is the stage that most children go through in learning to read when most of their energy is focused on decoding the symbols that make up our script, rather than on understanding meaning. It is characterized by slow-and-hes-it-ant-read-ing.

the most important things you can do as a reader is thus to access as much of what you already know as possible, in order that important new knowledge and information, ways of thinking and arguing that you glean from texts can become integrated with the vast range of things you already know. If out of the interaction of what you already know and what you read come some new ideas, so much the better.

## Evaluate the author's success in communicating her ideas

As well as being about the attempt to understand what authors intended to convey, active reading also involves the attempt to evaluate how successful they are. As you read, ask yourself whether the author is clear. If she is, try to work out what has led to this clarity. Does it result from brevity, or from a good choice of words, for example? If the author is unclear, try to work out what she might do to make herself clearer. Is her language unclear? Or has she failed to give you all the information you need?

Whenever you read you should evaluate the arguments – the reasoning and evidence – that authors give to support their points of view. Try to ensure, if you use what others have written in directly defending or building your own point of view, that there is some real justification for doing so. The fact that you find an author's ideas attractive and feel inclined to agree with them does not mean that she has argued well. This might seem obvious, but more people than you might believe possible fail to notice the seductive way in which finding that an author goes along with one's own point of view can numb the ability to notice that she is arguing badly.

If an author uses examples and illustrations, are they interesting and pertinent? If she cites evidence, ask yourself whether it is good enough. Is it strong and to the point? Sometimes authors cite as evidence, facts that are in themselves interesting and might have been strong evidence in favour of a variety of other conclusions, but are only marginally relevant to the argument they are attempting to present. Such evidence should not sway you, however interesting you find it in its own right. Consider, for example, an author who argued, at the start of the year 2000, that the Labour Government was highly successful, because it had an overwhelming majority in the House of Commons. Though this argument might have had some attraction for those who had a vested interest in portraying the Labour regime as successful, it could not have been expected to persuade anyone with any power to reason, because the size of a government's majority in itself says nothing at all about how successful it is.

## Engage with the author

Whenever you read academically, you should engage with the text and thus strike up some kind of relationship with its author. It can be useful to imagine, as you read, that she is sitting beside you. What images come to mind as you read her work that you would like to share with her? What feelings does her work evoke in you, that you feel it would be right to share? What questions would you want to ask? What suggestions would you like to make about ways of improving her text? What do you know that she might find useful in developing her ideas or stating them more clearly? Have you read anything that you think she should read? Why?

## Decide on further reading

Active reading will always involve the attempt to decide whether you should read more in relation to your topic, and if so, what. You may decide that you need to read more in order to allow you to understand some point or argument that the author is making. Sometimes this might involve reading sources to which she refers, but sometimes, and perhaps especially when you are reading longer texts like books, you may find yourself wanting to read other parts of the same book; or to reread what you have already read, more methodically. In some instances you will want to pursue further evidence to support or substantiate a claim made by an author; in others you might want, in addition, to check her use of sources.

For some people the idea of having to revisit passages that they read hours or even days earlier will suggest failure – as if they didn't do a good enough job first time round. They are mistaken. Academic reading is difficult and it will hardly ever be possible to grasp the whole meaning of a text in one reading. Moving backwards and forwards through a text is part of the process of reading actively – especially when you find yourself wanting to check again on what an author has said earlier. The author may even suggest that this will be helpful, for example by writing, 'I want now to make use of an argument I developed earlier . . .', or 'Towards the end of this article, I will make use of this idea in addressing . . .'.

### Approach the text with questions: decide what you want to get from it

Before beginning to read any text, ask yourself questions such as these:

- What do I hope to gain from reading this text?
- What questions can it help me to answer?
- How much time do I intend to spend reading it?
- Do I want to record what I find out and, if so, how should I do it?

Your answers to these questions will depend partly on your reasons for reading and partly upon how familiar you are with the material. They should help to form the ways in which you read. For example, if the text is new to you, it will probably be best to begin in an exploratory way by undertaking a kind of reconnaissance mission. On the other hand, if it is a text you know already, you may be looking for particular bits of information and have a good idea where they are to be found.

Some students develop the unfortunate belief that whenever they read they should be trying, as far as possible, to remember everything the author has written. Such students will often read as if they are compelled to read every word. Their vision focuses on individual ideas in a way that does not allow them to notice the grand scale of the entire forest of ideas. In other words, they can't see the wood for the trees, never mind taking account of individual specimens – their species, size, age, form and state of health. In reading you have to be able to move in and out of various levels of focus. You need to be able, not only to see the wood as a whole and its relationship to the intellectual landscape around it, but also to examine things at the level of the individual tree or argument, and even at the level of the individual bud or leaf – the ideas and premises, the facts and opinions, that go to make up whole arguments, theses, theories and world views.

### Have specific questions in mind as you read

You must keep reminding yourself that your reading can be made more purposeful by having specific questions in mind. What do you want to learn from this text and about this text? Bear in mind that as you read your list of questions may change, either because you rejig the individual questions, or because you find new questions coming to mind. It can be useful to stop every so often to assess how well you are managing to find answers to your questions; in any case, when you have read the entire text you should consider whether or not they have been answered and, if necessary, make notes about what you have learned. Finally, you may want to consider whether there is anything to be gained by formulating new questions and rereading in a more detailed way.

### SQ3R: Survey, Question, Read, Recite, Review[14]

We have discussed some ways of making your reading more effective by focusing on your purposes, and on the need to read actively and with particular questions in mind. If you feel the need for more structure, you will probably find it useful to apply a systematized reading technique known as *SQ3R (Survey, Question, Read, Recite, Review;* Beard 1987). Though it can make the

---

14 Our discussion of SQ3R is very brief; if you wish to consider it in more detail, you will find it mentioned in many guides to study skills, including *Reading, Writing and Reasoning* (Fairbairn and Winch 1996) where you will find some detailed examples.

process of getting to grips with a text look easier than it actually is, *SQ3R* can be useful for those who like the security of a definite pattern, and even those who feel constrained, rather than enabled, by systematic approaches will find the steps as listed useful, provided that they give themselves permission to move between them as often as they like, and in whatever order suits them best.

Essentially, *SQ3R* lists the different activities in reading that we have discussed, in a series of five steps.

### Survey

Begin by surveying the text to get a general idea of what it is about. This should help you to decide how helpful it might be for your purposes. In doing so, you should use the structural features of the text – contents list, index, list of key words, summaries etc.

### Question

Next, you should make the attempt to become clear about what it is you want to get from this text, formulating questions with which to approach it. What do you want to know? Where in the text are you likely to find it? As you read, and gain information from the text, you should modify and refine your questions.

### Read

Next, read the text in whatever ways are most helpful. Does it contain the information you need? Some of the time you will be scanning for information, sometimes you will skim sections, and at other times you will slow right down, reading slowly and carefully to allow you to absorb and understand detailed arguments. You will find this stage more productive if you have prepared the way well through the first stages. Some people will want to take notes as they read. We would advise you to leave note taking until the next stage, when you have more idea of what it is that you wish to take notes about.

### Recite (or recall)

What have you learned? Having worked out what you want
to find out and attempted to locate it in the text, now is
the time to stop and think about what you have learned –
literally to recall it and recite it to yourself. Have you found
answers to your questions? This is probably the ideal time
to take notes about what you have learned.

### Review

Now look over the text again, to make sure that you haven't
missed anything important. Have you found what you
wanted? Make sure that you have gleaned everything you
can from this text that will help to answer the questions
you set at the beginning. Now look to the future. What
should you do next? Is there more reading to be done? Will
you have to look at your notes again soon, to ensure that
you retain what you have gained?

Often you will need to read and reread a passage several times
until you are satisfied that you understand it and all its implica-
tions. Rereading a passage is only very rarely about simply reading it for a second or third time. More likely is that you will do
so with different questions in mind than those with which you
approached it on the first occasion – filling in gaps, making sure
that you understood things correctly, checking out details. In
addition, during the second and subsequent readings you are
likely to want to focus on sections that you found particularly
difficult during the first reading as, in a sense, you become more
of an expert on its subject matter.

## 'Having' and 'being': two ways of approaching reading[15]

Barnes (1995) talks about two ways of interacting with texts:
'learning the text' and 'learning from the text'. He argues that

---

15 We should point out that our discussion here is necessarily somewhat sparse
and you may wish to read what Barnes has written about this topic in his
book *Successful Study for Degrees* (1995) which we enjoyed very much and
which first drew our attention to this idea from Fromm.

those who incline towards 'learning the text' are predisposed to commit the text and what it says to memory. More useful is 'learning from the text', which focuses on understanding what the text is about. We think a third approach, 'learning about the text', lies between these two. It is about developing sufficient familiarity with a text to allow you to know both what you would want to learn from it and where you might want to learn the text itself. For example, where an author has said something particularly well (or badly) you might decide that it is worth committing her words to memory, or at least recording them to allow you to quote them in an essay at a later point.

Barnes relates his discussion to Fromm's suggestion that students' attitudes to their work can influence their ability to study. In his book *To Have or to Be?* (1979) Fromm made a distinction between two approaches to learning, which he labelled respectively as the 'having' and 'being' modes of learning. He argued that the belief that it is possible to 'have' knowledge constituted a block to the ability to study; Barnes relates this to 'learning the text'. Ask yourself whether it applies to you. For example, when you read a book, do you do so thinking that you can somehow extract its goodness – the information or knowledge it contains – in much the same way that you might visit a shop to buy a new CD? If this is the way you approach reading you may fall prey to the temptation merely to store up all the new knowledge you accrue, in a kind of mental library or database from which, with luck, you can retrieve it at will. The problem with this approach to texts is that it may lead you to fail in really coming to understand or even getting to know, in the sense of 'becoming familiar with', the texts that you read. If your aim is merely to capture ideas from them, so that you can store them ready for regurgitation in essays and assignments, you may fail to interact with them – questioning them and conversing with them in such a way that you come to really *own* the ideas that you harvest – because by pushing them about a bit, you have made them your own. Students who take the 'having' approach to reading will often fail to note that 'between the lines' of any book, article or passage there may be a hidden text – hidden layers of meaning, including assumptions that underpin arguments, and nuances that the author has chosen not to state.

Students who approach reading in the 'being' mode, who in Barnes's terms aim to 'learn from the text', are more likely to engage with the text, to allow themselves to be stimulated by its arguments and suggestions, to relate what is said to what they already know, believe and feel. Such students, in other words, are more likely to absorb relevant and useful aspects of the text into their everyday life, so that they become part of the ways in which they make sense of and understand the world. Reading actively, in the way we have suggested you should do in Part 4, is clearly aligned to the 'being' mode and Barnes's idea of learning from the text. However, rather than just learning from the text, we have been trying to suggest that, where possible, you should learn *with* the text, engaging with it and its author in a conversation designed to grow your current knowledge and understanding through interaction with new ideas.

# PART 5: Deciding what to read

A good reader will be able to use a range of approaches to reading, and will possess a variety of helpful reading skills. Perhaps even more importantly, a good reader will be able to make sensible decisions about what reading will be worthwhile. In Part 5, we discuss ways in which you might make such decisions.

## WHAT TO READ: TEXTBOOKS OR ACADEMIC BOOKS AND ARTICLES?

The people who teach you will influence what you read, through reading they set or suggest in connection with their classes. Perhaps most importantly, they will influence your reading by making interesting references to authors from whom they have drawn in developing their own ideas and views and also (if you are lucky) to authors who disagree with their views. A lecturer who exudes enthusiasm for her subject can make the difference between a student who hardly opens a book and one who reads avidly.

As a student you will have to read textbooks. These usually aim to teach about an academic area by offering an introduction or overview. However, you will also have to read specialist academic books and articles which will usually be more demanding, have a narrower focus and be aimed at communicating original ideas and research to professional academics and researchers.

As you progress with your studies, you should be reading fewer student textbooks, and more original academic work. This is not to say that textbooks are not worthwhile, and in most disciplines there are some that help to shape generations of academics. However, even in the early stages of your course, you should beware of falling into the trap of believing that textbooks always present the definitive word on a topic. They may give less detail than you will need in writing essays; they may contain inaccuracies. Perhaps more importantly, even the best textbooks are likely to be out of date in relation to some things, since they cannot be updated sufficiently frequently to take account of the most recent theoretical work and research. For some disciplines this is a significant problem, especially in the sciences. Not only that, but you will often find that textbook authors emphasize different things and disagree with one another about important points of detail. That is one reason that you should be aware of the need, if possible, to follow up the references that they make to primary and other sources.

The decision about whether to read textbooks or more specialist sources will depend on your level of study, the amount of detail that is necessary for your purposes, and your previous knowledge and experience. When you are new to an area, textbooks may be the best way to gain an overview. However, even as an undergraduate, regurgitating information you have derived from such sources will rarely be good enough in itself.

## WHERE SHOULD YOU BEGIN TO READ WHEN YOU ARE READING FOR AN ASSIGNMENT?

Some lecturers will give out suggestions for specific reading in relation to your assignments, and you may even be given prescribed reading. This can be helpful, but it won't be if you can't get hold of the material that is prescribed or recommended.

This is a common experience, as you either know or will soon discover.

Other students can be a good source of ideas for reading, especially when they have already done an assignment on the same topic or in the same area, as might be the case if you are lucky enough to make friends with someone who is on the same course but a year ahead of you. The notes you take in lectures may well give you some guidance about reading that will be worthwhile, especially if you are in the fortunate position of having a lecturer who is undertaking research in areas about which you are asked to write for an assignment. In this case you may find that during their classes they make references to material that is really up to date and relevant. Such references are likely to be far more useful than references in a reading list that may have been around for some time and perhaps for some years.

## Using reading lists

Some of your lecturers will provide a list of suggested reading in relation to every assignment they set. What items on such a list should you read first? Should you bother with reading lists at all? In practice you will probably read whatever you can lay your hands on – but what should you read first if you can get a hold of everything? A number of factors might influence such decisions, including how easily you can access listed texts, and whether those you can get hold of look inviting or boring. You may also be influenced by the fame or, in some cases, the notoriety of authors, and by the style in which they write – whether their texts are highly technical or written in easy prose. In subjects that depend on ongoing research, especially of an empirical kind, the age of the material will be important because the more recent it is, the more likely it is that you will be able to pick up clues to other interesting and hopefully important up-to-date work that you should read.

### What do reading lists list?

A surprisingly high number of students seem to be rather indiscriminating when it comes to deciding what to read. For example, many – at least when they are in the early part of their course – naïvely believe that the fact that a book or article has made it on to a reading list means that it is worth reading. They may well believe that they are expected to read their way through the entire reading list as part of their course and that, if they do not do so, they will somehow be failing.

What matters is that such students have somehow developed the idea that among books and sources on their subject, those that appear on the 'reading list' are somehow magically endowed with qualities that will enable students who study them to attain higher grades. As a result, and unless they have already developed worthwhile skills and disciplines as readers, they may buy or borrow one or more of the books on the list and begin to read it; what's more, they may well try to read it from cover to cover, from beginning to end – all the way through, with no reason for doing so other than that it appears on *THE READING LIST*.

### So what do reading lists list?

Perhaps it's over-sceptical of us to say as much in a book that we hope will be read by countless students, but in our view reading lists are often a waste of time. Certainly it is rarely the case that students will have to read all of the books and other texts that appear on a reading list in order to achieve success. If particular texts are so important that the course depends on them, it is likely that this will be indicated – 'Books marked by an * are essential/required reading.' That kind of thing.

So how should you use a reading list? Should you try to read all of the books and other texts, one by one? Should you focus mainly on those that are labelled as essential or required reading? The first of these ideas is plainly silly; if you follow that route when you meet a reading list, you are destined to waste time. If books really are essential reading there will be some genuine reason why this is so. If they are labelled in this way, you should ask your lecturers for guidance about why it is essential for you to read them. What, for example, should you expect to get from reading them? Ask whether it is essential for you to read the whole book, or only certain sections, because it is obviously better for you to spend focused time on those, than to read the whole thing in a superficial way (look again at the quotation from Woody Allen on page 46).

Unless you have good reason to believe that it really is essential to read particular items, the best way to think of reading lists is perhaps to view them as a very selected library of relevant books on which you may wish to graze. Then, when you have time, you can select a few from those on offer, reading what's relevant or more importantly what interests you or even excites or enthralls you, following up the clues that authors give to other material that might be more interesting and even more useful.

You should not panic if you find that you cannot understand a word of a book or article that you have decided really is essential reading, or if it turns out to be so boring that you keep falling asleep while trying to read it. Remember that time spent on a text that you can't understand, or find boring beyond belief, is time wasted – unless, that is, you manage, through failing to read it, to work out what you will have to do in order to be able to understand it. In general, it is better to find and read some other book or article on the same theme that does interest you. Of course, if the experience of not understanding, or of being bored by what you read, becomes too common, so that you keep having to look for alternatives, you may conclude that the trouble lies with you and not with the particular text or texts you are having difficulty in reading.

You might reasonably expect and hope that your lecturers will only include books on reading lists because they are the most important, the most relevant, the best written, the most thoroughly researched texts available in a subject or on a particular topic. Unfortunately, this is rarely the case. Reading lists are sometimes not updated as often as they might be and sometimes they are thrown together hastily and under pressure. Sometimes lecturers place books on a reading list because they are the only relevant (or kind of relevant) books that sprang to mind when they were asked to supply a renewed reading list just before leaving for their summer holidays, or even worse, just before the start of the new university year. Sometimes, in other words, the items on a reading list are not chosen on merit but because, like Everest, they just happened to be there.

No doubt some lecturers will list the best books available – in their view. But even in such cases it is worth noticing that since lecturers, like you, are only human, their suggestions for crucially important reading may be nothing of the kind. And so even if they have done their best (and most university teachers probably do their best most of the time), there may still be other sources that will suit you better as a reader and as a learner.

## IS IT WORTH READING? USING THE STRUCTURAL FEATURES OF ACADEMIC TEXTS

In Part 1 we described the process by which our daughter makes decisions about whether a story book is worth reading; and in Part 4 we described the way in which a friend who left school at 14 approaches newspapers and magazines, using features such as headlines, contents lists and pictures to make decisions about what he wants to read. We want, now, to focus on the ways in which you make such decisions.

---

**How do you decide whether to read a book?**　　*Task 5.1*

Imagine that you have been set an essay on a topic with which you are unfamiliar, and that you have decided to look at a number of books as a first attempt to familiarize yourself with the area. Whether you have decided to look at these books because they have been suggested by a lecturer or a friend, or because you have come across references to them, the first thing you will have to do is to decide how much time it is worth investing in them. How would you do this?

Take a few minutes to reflect on the ways in which you make decisions about which books to read. Do you use the structural features of texts in making decisions? Do you do so in a disciplined or organized way?

---

If you have a strategy for making decisions about what is worth reading, how did you come to have it? Did you develop it yourself? Or were you, like Faith, taught it in school?

## Using the structural features of books

Academic books have a range of features that can be useful in assessing their relevance for your purposes, and the likelihood that they are reliable and/or original contributions to their field.

### *Title, blurb, publishing history*

The *title* and, where there is one, the *subtitle* of a book will often give some indication of its topic. However, it is as well to be aware that authors sometimes hit on titles more because they are likely to attract readers than because they give an accurate indication of the book's contents. This is also true of the description of the book which appears as the *blurb* on the back page or, in the case of a hardback book, on the inside flap of the dustjacket. Like the title and cover design, blurbs are intended by publishers to act as bait in attracting readers. However, they will often give an overview of the book's contents or at least point to some of its main ideas.

Often you will find comments about a book on its back cover. Such comments take two forms. Some are extracted from reviews of the book which have appeared in journals; others are more like 'testimonials' which have been solicited from well-known academics who are likely to be sympathetic to its style and content, and thus to say nice things about it. Both are intended to interest you in the book, and they are likely to be highly selective. A publisher is much more likely to print '. . . an extremely readable book which provides a detailed and original examination of this topic' on the back of a book than 'It is turgid, poorly researched and does little to advance knowledge.' Nonetheless, the fact that a book has been well received by some people suggests that it is at least worth taking seriously, though the extent to which you act upon their praise may depend on what you know about those whose opinion you are reading.

You may want to check whether the book is in a second or subsequent edition and whether it has been reprinted; these details will be found, almost invariably on the reverse of the title page of the book, along with details of the publisher, the date of publication and the ISBN number. Although they do not prove that it is worthwhile, the fact that a book has been reprinted or published in a revised edition at least indicates that it has had a certain measure of success. The date of publication may also help you to decide how useful a book will be – especially, for example, in the sciences and social sciences, where rapid changes in both theory and practice are common.

## Contents, preface, acknowledgements, foreword

The *contents page* will give you some idea of the book's scope, depending on the level of detail provided, which can vary from a simple list of chapter headings to a list of chapters along with the main headings in each. You will often be able to tell at a glance whether there are whole chapters that address the topics in which you are interested.

In some books you will also find a *preface and/or acknowledgements* section near the front, which can be helpful, because they may tell you something about the author's reasons for writing the book. Acknowledgements are sometimes an excuse for authors to indulge in a spot of 'name-dropping', suggesting that their book is important because such prestigious and famous people were involved with them while they were writing it. However, depending on what they actually say, acknowledgements can be helpful, along with other features of a book, in assessing whether it is a serious contribution to the literature especially where, for example, what is acknowledged is the specific contribution that an individual has made in relation to a technical or professional matter in which they are an acknowledged authority.

In addition to a preface, some books have a *foreword*, written by someone other than the author, which may give an indication of significant parts of the content. Forewords often serve as testimonials to a book's importance and they always merit consideration, because they are likely to be written by people of some stature, whose views we might wish to take seriously. However, it is worth bearing in mind that, as with blurbs and the extracts from reviews that appear on the back covers of books, publishers are unlikely to print a foreword that is adversely critical of an author and her work.

## *Index*

Perhaps the best guide to a book's value is the *index*, which should provide an overview of topics, along with an indication of the main pages where they are to be found. Most serious academic books, unless they are quite old, will have an index and sometimes two – one to cover ideas and concepts, and one to cover authors cited in the text. Books that lack a decent index are likely to be less helpful than those that do – certainly they are less user friendly, and for that reason rather irritating.

There are some important points that you should bear in mind, when you are looking through a book's index. First, its main topic may not be listed because the whole text is viewed as being about that topic. Secondly, the topics or issues in which you are interested may appear under different headings that overlap to some extent. Thus, for example, if you were interested in responsibility, you might also look under entries for related terms such as 'accountability', 'duty', 'liability' and 'obligation', all of which can be used synonymously with 'responsibility' in some of its senses; and if you are interested in suicide you might want to look up 'self-murder', 'self-harm', 'parasuicide', 'euthanasia' and 'cry for help', because to some extent all overlap with common ideas about suicide.

## *Reference list/bibliography*

The last structural element to which you should turn your attention is the *reference list* in which, if she has adopted the Harvard system for citation (or some variation of it), the author will give details of sources; sometimes such a list is called a bibliography. Reference lists (or bibliographies) of work cited are usually collected in one list near the end of the book, though they may be gathered at the end of each chapter, especially in the case of edited books. They will often give you a good indication about the range of influences that have contributed to the development of the author's ideas and, where this matters, will allow you to gauge how up-to-date her knowledge of the literature is. Sometimes a book's reference list will lead you to other sources that you will decide to consult even if, in the end, you do not read the book.

In addition to giving references to work cited, some academic books, usually those that are written as textbooks, will contain a list of other work in the field. Such lists are labelled in different ways, including 'Suggestions for further reading' and, somewhat confusingly, they are sometimes called 'Bibliographies'. Such a list may also guide you towards worthwhile reading.

## Layout

Finally, after looking at the front cover; blurb; contents list; preface and acknowledgements; reference list/bibliography and index, you may want to consider the layout of the book before at last turning to the text. For example, does it contain diagrams, tables or illustrations and do they look helpful/difficult? Does it contain easily identifiable overviews or summaries that will help you to assess, and even absorb, the relevance of the content?

---

### Gutting a book

Our friend Albert Radcliffe, whose metaphor of the reader as a cloakroom attendant we discussed in Part 2, talked to us about an occasion, as a theology student, when a tutor offered him help in getting to grips with a particularly large and difficult text. The tutor's advice was that he should 'gut' the book.

Since Albert first shared this metaphor with us, we have noticed it being used by a number of people. It is very rich. Gutting a book implies getting right into the middle of it and throwing away what you don't want. There are obvious variations. Filleting a book, for example, might involve removing the bones, locating and retaining the backbone (the central arguments and themes), and discarding all the irritating little bones – the irrelevant ideas that might stick in your throat and cause confusion in both understanding what was being said and in constructing your own arguments. Filleting and gutting a fish can take some time, but doing so may make it easier to eat. Filleting and gutting a book is even more time consuming, but it will help you to decide both whether it has any merit and which parts you want to attempt to digest first.

---

## Using the structural features of journals and journal articles

Like books, articles in academic journals also have organizational features which can help you in assessing where you should invest your time and effort. For example, one common feature is an *abstract* at the beginning of each article – a brief account of the main points – which should help you to reach a reasoned decision about whether the article is worth reading. In addition, many journals give lists of key words for each article, which will help you to assess whether it is of interest. Finally, it is worth looking at the references cited. This can give some impression of the article's scope and of how aware the author is of important texts and, perhaps even more than in the case of books, references cited may prove a useful source of further avenues for research.

---

| **Dissecting journal articles** | *Task 5.2* |
|---|---|

Visit your institutional library or some other library that has decent stocks of journals on topics in which you have an interest. Find a journal that interests you and browse quickly through some of the copies that the library holds. Then select a single issue of that journal and spend no more than an hour reading four of the articles as quickly as possible. Use the structural features of the articles to get an overview of their key messages along with anything that confuses you or that you don't understand, and any references to other literature that you might like to follow up.

In carrying out this task you should try to avoid the attempt to read the article in detail – first look at the list of key words, then read the abstract and the conclusion, then read the first paragraph and scan any headings and subheadings. Finally skim through the article taking in as much as possible, without reading every word.

---

This task is worth practising as often as possible – both as a form of limbering up if you have no specific reading to be getting on with (which is an unlikely state of affairs) and in relation to writing and other tasks that you are set by your teachers. It can help you to develop the techniques and disciplines and stamina that are necessary for reviewing the literature in an area, in order to gain a broad sweep of current ideas in a particular field. With practice you should be able to double the number of articles you can dissect in an hour. The more efficiently you can gauge the main points of an article from a brief scanning, the greater the amount of time you will have to read articles that you are seriously interested in, in depth.

# PART 6: Reading and note taking

In Parts 3 and 4 we talked about improving your reading by changing the ways in which you think about it and by developing specific reading skills. In Part 5, we continued this theme by offering some advice about ways of taking control over decisions about what you should read. Our aim is to help you to become a more active reader, engaging with the authors whose work you read, rather than merely feeding off them, absorbing what they say. In Part 6 we continue this discussion by talking about note taking and its relationship to active reading.

## NOTE TAKING AS A STUDENT READER

As a student you will be expected to remember, organize and make use of enormous amounts of information, most of which will probably come from your reading. Some will be the kind of information that we commonly refer to as 'knowledge', implying that there is a certain definiteness about it, or that it makes so much sense that people accept it as true. Other information that you will be expected to acquire and use will not be knowledge.

Rather it will take the form of opinions and points of view. When you take notes, you will have to find ways of distinguishing between these different kinds of information.

---

**Why take notes when reading?**                    *Task 6.1*

Write down as many reasons as you can for taking notes when you are reading. Try to do this without looking at the purposes for note taking that we outline below.

---

The range of reasons that people have (or think they have) for writing notes is huge. For example, you may make notes in order:

- to help you to remember the main points in the text/to jog your memory later (can you see the difference?)
- to give you ready access to particular facts and arguments in an easier form
- to link new knowledge to what you already know
- to help you to understand what an author is saying
- to make a record of points that you might want to use in an essay.

Sometimes books or articles will strike you as so important, or so interesting, that they will stick in your memory without your recording them. However, it is probably always best to work on the assumption that unless you record what you have read, you are going to forget it, or that, even if you remember it, you are likely to forget that you do. Memory is a complex business. We do not usually remember the two times table when we are driving down the road, or a poem that we committed to memory as children when we are watching television. And unless we do some work in securing its memory, we may not remember what we have learned from a text.

### The mindless note taker

Authors of books about study skills (and there are many of them) often claim that taking notes as you read will force you to think about what you are reading, as if this is a reason for taking notes. They are wrong. Note taking can help you to focus on what you read, but it can only do so if you remain aware of what you are taking notes about and why. Unfortunately many students take notes that seem to have gone directly from the page they are reading, through their eyes, then via their hand to their note pad or computer, without passing anywhere near their mind. As a result they often end up with pages of notes that they do not understand, about something they have barely read.

Have you ever found yourself telling a friend that you have just spent two hours taking notes for an essay from a set text, but that you still haven't got the foggiest idea of what it is about? Avoid this all too common experience by making sure that you think carefully about your purpose not only in reading but in taking notes. As with all other aspects of reading, the most important thing about note taking is that you should engage your brain: mindless note taking is generally bad note taking. Be discriminating, whatever style of note taking you favour. Try to ensure that the notes you make will help you to recall not only the information the author is seeking to convey and her views, but your reactions to what she has to say.

Reading actively, always attempting to relate what you read to what you know, will help you to avoid the possibility of becoming a mindless note taker. For example, you might note points of comparison between an author's claims and claims made by others, or between her arguments and those used by others. If you do cross refer like this you must be clear about why you are doing so; writing, for example, 'See also Bloggs (1998)' isn't enough – because by the time you come to reread your notes, you may have forgotten who Bloggs is.

## HOW DO YOU TAKE NOTES?

Some people take notes as they read, while others do so afterwards, and there are huge variations in the ways in which people actually write notes. Let's have a look at your note taking.

---

**How do you take notes when reading?**          *Task 6.2*

Think a little about how you take notes when you are reading.
Then reflect on the questions below.

---

Do you take notes with the book or other text open? Do you
take notes as you read, or do you read first and return to
take notes during a second or even third reading? Do you
perhaps take brief notes as you read and fill them out later?

Do you ever take notes with the book or other text closed,
then check what you have written by rereading relevant
passages?

What form do your textual notes take? Are they different
from your notes on lectures?

Do you take linear notes – like a condensed version of the
original? Do you write them in your own words – using
your own authorial voice? Or do you copy bits of what the
author has said? Do you ensure that you distinguish her
words and your own? How?

Do you take pictorial or diagrammatic notes?

Do you key word?

Do you rework your notes later? For example, do you transfer
key words and main ideas to index cards or to computer
files?

Are you careful, however you take notes, to keep an accurate
bibliographical record of each source, including the pages
on which quotations are to be found? How do you do it?
In a big notebook? On index cards? Using a computer
database?

---

**Note taking that suits your own learning style**

The form of note taking you adopt will depend to some extent
on your learning style and the ways in which you think. While
some people stick rigidly to one approach to taking notes, others

will develop a mixed economy of note taking, using diagrammatic notes for ideas that ask to be noted in that way, while giving in to those ideas that demand to be noted down in the form of a list – whether of key words, short notes or sentences, and those that ask to be written about more extensively. Importantly, the way in which you choose to take notes will depend on the material that you are reading and on the particular purposes that you have both in reading and in writing notes. For example, it might be most appropriate to take notes about a complex argument in a linear style – each stage of the argument appearing on a new line. On the other hand, notes about, for example, a scientific process, the relationship between the various individuals in an organization, or the causes of a historical event, may be best recorded pictorially or diagrammatically.

## APPROACHING NOTE TAKING IN DIFFERENT WAYS

Though we shall talk about different approaches, we do not intend to give detailed instructions about taking notes, because we think that the most important thing is that you should develop a style that suits you. As a general rule of thumb, whatever approach you adopt, the more effort you put into your notes – the more you work them and rework them, making the words in which they are written and the ways in which they are written your own – the more meaningful and useful you will find them. Remember that in order to record what you read, you need not write it down in detail, but may instead write a few key ideas or words that will serve to jog your memory when you want to remember and make use of what you know.

You may well have received some instruction in note taking at school or college, but if you didn't, and want to learn more about different ways of taking notes than you can gather from this book, you might want to browse through the shelves in your university library or local bookshop. In the meantime, we want to invite you to read and take notes on a short passage, from a popular science book which raises many interesting questions through a critique of the science behind the popular Jurassic Park movies.

| Practising note taking: *The Science of Jurassic Park and the Lost World* | Task 6.3 |
|---|---|

Read the passage below and take notes of a kind that will help you to recall its most important points and to offer some critique if called upon to do so.

The velociraptors of *Jurassic Park* and *The Lost World* are an odd case. They're greedy, selfish, and aggressive – aggressive toward each other and even toward their own infants. On the other hand, they're also skillful pack hunters and appear to put their rivalries aside while chasing their prey: one raptor will maneuver a weak, straying triceratops away from its herd while another waits in hiding to pounce on the prey. But how did orphan raptors acquire the cooperative skills needed for hunting while remaining completely devoid of the similarly cooperative skills needed for living and surviving in a pack? In particular, the idea that raptors would deny food to their own infants is difficult to believe. Most animals display a distinctive protectiveness toward their offspring – their own offspring, at least. Without this instinct, no species is likely to survive. Who knows what basic survival skills mother dinosaurs, or a herd of adult dinosaurs, would have taught dinosaur youngsters? Surprisingly, paleontologists have been able to make a few simple inferences about the way some dinosaurs raised their young. Jack Horner, uncovering the nest sites of great herds of maiasaurs on the North American plains, discovered bones of juveniles, up to a moderate size, either at or near the nests. It seems reasonable to guess that the maiasaur parents kept their offspring near the nest and fed them until the youngsters reached the point of self-sufficiency, rather than abandoning them as soon as they were hatched. But did both parents look after the children, or just the mothers? Did parents look after only their own children, or did they form cooperative nursing groups? Those questions are harder to answer.

DeSalle, R. and Lindley, D. (1997) *The Science of Jurassic Park and the Lost World – Or – How to Build a Dinosaur*. London. Harper Collins, pp.149–50.

What form did your notes take? For example, did you copy out sections of text, or render some of what the author said into your own words? Did you try to condense the passage? Did you make a note of questions that occurred to you as you read? Did you:

- write several lines of text (perhaps including numbered points and questions)?
- note down key words?
- make a diagram showing the relationships between ideas?

We found this passage interesting. However, as you will no doubt realize, it is not easy to write notes about it, because it is unclear how much of what is said is factual and how much is the result of speculation on the part of the authors. In trying to take notes about what DeSalle and Lindley are saying, we first of all went through the text underlining parts.

The <u>velociraptors</u> of *Jurassic Park* and *The Lost World* are an odd case. They're <u>greedy</u>, <u>selfish</u>, and <u>aggressive</u> – aggressive <u>toward each other</u> and <u>even</u> toward their <u>own infants</u>. On the other hand, they're also <u>skilful pack hunters</u> and appear to <u>put</u> their <u>rivalries aside</u> while <u>chasing</u> their <u>prey</u>: one raptor will <u>maneuver</u> a <u>weak, straying triceratops away from</u> its <u>herd while another waits</u> in hiding <u>to pounce</u> on the prey. But <u>how</u> did <u>orphan raptors acquire</u> the <u>cooperative skills</u> needed <u>for hunting</u> while remaining completely devoid of the similarly cooperative skills needed for living and surviving in a pack? In particular, the idea <u>that raptors would deny food to</u> their <u>own infants</u> is <u>difficult to believe</u>. Most animals display a distinctive protectiveness toward their offspring – their own offspring, at least. Without this instinct, no species is likely to survive. Who knows what basic survival skills mother dinosaurs, or a herd of adult dinosaurs, would have taught dinosaur youngsters? Surprisingly, <u>paleontologists</u> have been <u>able</u> to <u>make</u> a <u>few simple inferences about</u> the <u>way</u> some <u>dinosaurs raised</u> their <u>young</u>. Jack <u>Horner, uncovering</u> the <u>nest sites</u> of great herds <u>of maiasaurs</u> on the North American plains, <u>discovered bones</u> of <u>juveniles</u>, up to a <u>moderate size</u>, either <u>at or near</u> the <u>nests</u>. It seems <u>reasonable</u> to <u>guess that</u> the <u>maiasaur parents kept</u> their offspring near the nest and fed them until the youngsters reached the point of self-sufficiency, rather than abandoning them as soon as they were hatched. But did both parents look after the children, or just the mothers? Did parents look after only their own children, or did they form cooperative nursing groups? Those questions are harder to answer.

You might like to give some thought to how we could best organize our underlinings in a coherent form.

## Underlining/highlighting and making notes on the text

Instead of writing notes away from the text, some people choose always to work directly on it as we have done above – underlining or highlighting words and writing comments in the margin. Some academics view this practice with deep moral disapproval. That is why we thought hard about suggesting that you should try out this way of recording your reading, which can help to establish a stronger relationship between you and the things you read. At first, in a wimpish moment, we thought of just sharing with you the fact that at times we both find it helpful to write in books, leaving you to come to your own conclusion about what to do. Since then we have had second thoughts. We now want to offer you our wholehearted endorsement of the practice of writing in books and other texts, because doing so is likely to help you to use them better, provided that you only ever write in materials that belong to you, and never in those that belong to others.

One of us developed the habit of writing in books when he was an Open University student. Much of the teaching on distance learning programmes like that run by the OU goes on through the medium of print, and in the past, before the development of the Internet, this was even more true. As a result, he found that the only way to engage properly with what his teachers – the authors of course units and texts – were saying seemed to be to respond to them directly. And so he began to interact with them (or at least with their words) by writing in margins, and underlining sections of text. His career as a book defiler carried on through his postgraduate studies and up to the present time, though nowadays his writing in books is more restrained.

What's more, he decided early on that it was best to write in pen, because using a more permanent medium seemed to show that he really meant business – that he really had something to say. This seemed better than making nervous and mean little pencil squiggles and notes, as if he wanted to apologize for having something to say. Gradually different colours of ink came into play – to mark different kinds of point, and to overwrite earlier marks. This can be helpful,[16] but it can also go wrong when you are first beginning to interact with books in this way. For example, as a result of his turbulent relationship with some books (combined with over-enthusiastic use of highlighting pens) Gavin felt compelled to buy more than one copy; he has three copies of the same edition of one book, each marked differently (and with varying colour schemes). As a result of his urge to engage with the authors he has read, some of the books on our shelves would be pretty much unreadable to anyone else. On the other hand, twenty years or so after writing in some of his books, those marks still mean something, and though some are now undecipherable, many still remind him of what he was thinking at the time.

Though you may well find it helpful to make marks on and write in the margins of books and photocopies that you own, you should be aware that it is probably better to refrain from doing so during your first reading of a text. This is especially true where you find yourself feeling outraged, annoyed or simply astonished by things that an author says. Just as your relationships with people you meet in the flesh will change over time, so might your relationships with authors and their books. Responding to a text by writing comments without first reflecting carefully about what the author has written can lead to unhelpful mess that you may regret later, perhaps as your views about an author's opinions or arguments mellow. It is always better to wait a bit and return to the text when you are able to be more

---

16 Some people use a range of colours to highlight points of different kinds. We draw this to your attention although neither of us could do it, because if you are able to work in the obsessional way that this practice demands, you might find it useful.

objectively critical, rather than taking the risk of messing a book up for ever by responding in the heat of the moment. Alternatively, this might be the time to write some notes directly into a word processing file in the kind of way that we describe on pages 114–16.

---

**Remember this**

Never mark or write in a book (or any other text) that belongs to someone else. To do so is ill-mannered and uncaring.

---

## Linear notes

Some people take linear notes – that is, notes that go in straight lines. Is this your preferred method of note taking?

---

**Notes on a passage from**                                    *Task 6.4*
*The Lopsided Ape* **(p.198)**

Have a look at the notes that follow and then turn to the passage about which they were made, which you will find on page 197, to see whether you think they represent it fairly. The passage is taken from *The Lopsided Ape: Evolution of the Generative Mind*, in which the author Corballis (1991) examines the importance, for human evolution, of laterality in the brain, that is, the fact that the right and left sides of the brain have different functions.

Are these notes adequate? Do they miss out any important details? How would you change them? Bear in mind that note taking is an individual business and what is adequate to remind one person about a text may be inadequate for someone else.

Left-handers not deficient in motor skills.

Peter and Servos distinguished between consistent and inconsistent L-handers.

Compared R and L-handers for skill, speed and strength (and speed of articulation and verbal fluency).

L-handers not inferior to R-handers in any test.

BUT inconsistents better with LH on fine motor skills.

AND better with RH on strength.

Conc: might cause problems where both strength and skill required.

Try writing your own notes on the passage.

### Key wording

Some people take very sparse notes which consist of little more than a list of key words, with occasional explanations, which are like condensed versions of the linear notes others might make. Using key words as a method of note taking involves making decisions that are similar to those you might have to make if you adopt the habit of underlining or highlighting text as you read.[17] Are you a key worder?

A disadvantage of key wording when compared with linear and diagrammatic notes is that they must be revisited and perhaps rewritten after a fairly short period, otherwise they may prove to be so thin on information as to be incomprehensible. Our advice to key wording note takers is to revisit your notes as soon as possible after making them, filling in details if necessary

---

17 Though they overlap, there is a difference between key wording as an approach to making notes about a text and reading for key words as a way of increasing your reading speed, which we discussed in Part 3. When you are reading a passage for the first time, the key words you look for will be those that are necessary to allow you to comprehend it. When you key word as a way of taking notes on a passage, on the other hand, the key words that you write down may be different, because they will be words that will help you to recall rather than merely understand. For one thing, you are likely to select fewer words, because by then you will know what the passage is about. If you are in the habit of underlining or highlighting key words directly on the text, what you do will be somewhere between these two, depending on whether you do so during your first or subsequent readings.

---

**Notes on a passage from *Education and***                    **Task 6.5**
***Personal Relationships* (p.31)**

---

The following notes have been made from a passage from *Education and Personal Relationships* by Downie, Loudfoot and Telfer (1974). The passage to which they refer, which can be found on page 197, is about the skills that go to make up the teacher's job.

Are these notes adequate? Do they cover everything the passage contains? Or do you think that they omit significant features?

*What skills make up teacher's job?*

*Teachers*

*Many different skills*

*Blackboard — detect restlessness/mutiny — story-telling — exciting/relevant*

*Colleges of Ed/headteachers*

*Age/stage pupils*

*'Skill-job' — set of skills*

*Teaching 'skill-job'*

*Musician: paradigm 'skill-job'*

*What skills make up teacher's job?*

---

but in any case reworking them to help establish their meaning and the connections that are necessary for remembering.

Rather than key wording directly, some people successively condense more detailed notes they have taken about a text into a series of key words, which can act as triggers to enable them to recall information that they have already absorbed. The advantage of having taken longer notes originally is that, if necessary, you can refer back to them again at a later stage. The process of condensing notes can, in itself, be helpful in locking the information they contain into your mind.

## Pictorial notes/web diagrams

Some people adopt a pictorial approach to note taking, drawing diagrams which connect ideas and facts together in 'spider's webs' of great complexity. They may use upper and lower case letters, underlining and a variety of colours to emphasize different aspects of their notes. Often in such diagrams, ideas gradually move out from a central concept, or perhaps from several concepts, with relationships between them shown by connecting lines; another refinement that some people use is to further establish the relationship between ideas by writing along the lines that connect them.

Some people will make use of other pictorial or diagrammatic devices. For example they may use flow charts – joining boxes that contain related ideas in a way that shows how one follows on from, or feeds into, another; they may draw pictures to remind them of certain ideas (this is quite different from 'aimless doodling'), and they may use Venn diagrams, or something similar, to show the relationships between ideas.

If you are not the kind of person who would naturally record ideas diagramatically or pictorially, it can be easy to dismiss this style of note taking as 'not for you'. If you are inclined to stick to linear note taking, we suggest that you do not dismiss diagramming out of hand, because you may find it beneficial for a number of reasons. For example, diagramming allows you to elaborate your notes later, adding further details and links; and you may find that it both helps you to see links and enables you to be creative in understanding and remembering texts.

---

| **Notes on a passage from *The True*** | **Task 6.6** |
| ***History of the Elephant Man* (p.20)** | |

Have a look at the diagrammatic notes that follow, which are based on a passage from *The True History of the Elephant Man* by Howell and Ford (1980). The passage from which these notes were made appears on page 198. Do you think they are a fair representation of its content? If they are inadequate, what would you do to make them better?

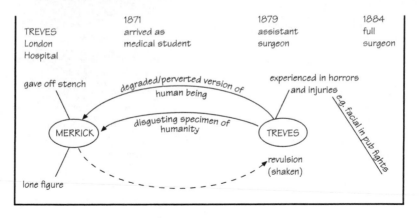

## COMPARING THE USEFULNESS OF LINEAR AND DIAGRAMMATIC NOTES

Now that we have said a little about a couple of different ways of making notes in relation to your reading, we would like you to attempt to make notes about two contrasting passages. They are, respectively, from a book about social science research methods, and from an article in a journal that has as its focus ethical issues in nursing.

---

**Linear versus diagrammatic/pictorial notes**          *Task 6.7*

In relation to each of the following passages, try making both linear and diagrammatic notes, then think about the difficulties and benefits of using each approach, given the texts, their styles and the authors' purposes. Notice whether you find yourself wanting to simply record what the authors have written, or whether, rather, you feel inclined to 'argue' with them – asking why they say the things they do and coming to a conclusion about whether they are justified in doing so. In general, do you think it is easier to take notes on a text with which you agree, or on one with which you disagree?

**Passage from Denscombe, M. (1998)** *The Good Research Guide.* **Buckingham: Open University Press, p.25.**
Traditionally, it is probability sampling which has set the standard for social research. It follows statistical laws and is well suited to the selection of samples in large-scale surveys designed to produce quantitative data. However, researchers who conduct small-scale research, especially qualitative researchers, find it difficult to adhere to the principles and procedures of probability sampling for selecting their people or events. Either it is not possible to include all types to be found in the population within a small sample, or not enough is known about the characteristics of the population to decide which people or events are suitable for inclusion in the sample. Some researchers have even attacked the principles of probability sampling as altogether inappropriate for smaller-scale, qualitative research. For these researchers, the selection of people or events for inclusion in the sample tends to be based on non-probability sampling.

The word 'tends' is quite important here. There is no absolute reason why qualitative research cannot use principles of randomness, or operate with large numbers. There are, however, some sound theoretical reasons why most qualitative research uses *non-probability sampling techniques* and good practical reasons why qualitative research deals with *small numbers* of instances to be researched.

**Passage from Hunt, G. (1999) 'Abortion: why bioethics can have no answer – a personal perspective',** *Nursing Ethics,* **6 (1): 47–57.**
Look at the things around you: a rock on the ground, a tree, a ring on my finger or a piece of furniture. Then turn the focus on yourself and ask yourself what they mean to you. A ring is not (just) a piece of metal; is it arbitrary or subjective to value this 'piece of metal' but not that one? I may describe it in that way (as just a piece of metal), and describing it so shows my attitude to it. I may be showing contempt for it. I feel nothing about the rock, but feeling nothing is my attitude and that is the importance of it: that I feel nothing about it. One may speak of an 'unborn child' or an 'embryo', of 'conception' or 'fertilization', of 'conceptus' or 'zygote', of 'baby' or 'fetus', of the 'baby's kick' or the 'fetal reflex', of a 'newborn' ('infant') or a 'neonate', but the contrast in each case is not between the moral/emotional and

the scientific/rational but between one set of reactions and attitudes and another. One is not superior to the other. They have different and, within the proper bounds, legitimate roles.

What is the difference between a gammon steak and slice of pig's buttock? Are they the same thing? Yes, but I'd rather have gammon with my peas and potatoes than a slice of pig's buttock. If I insist on seeing your gammon as a slice of pig's buttock then, surely, I am not just being 'more scientific' than you, I am making a point. You are not being 'irrational' or 'emotional' if you tell me to shut up. I am perhaps trying to disgust you to put you off, to incline you to vegetarianism.

What is meant by describing the signs we take to be significant as 'arbitrary' or 'subjective'? It has not escaped the notice of the perceptive bioethicist that there is no difference (scientifically, rationally) between a fetus just before and just after parturition. Thus, it follows, so it seems, that whatever it is acceptable to do to a fetus (baby?) one week before birth is acceptable to do one week after. We must accept this; reason demands it, or does it? If there is a difference in our attitude, is it explained by the fact that here there is an umbilical connection and here there is not? Our moral attitude cannot be reduced to any set of 'facts' at all.

## USING NOTE TAKING TO UNCOVER CONTENT

On pages 98–9 we said that we disagree with those who assume that taking notes about what you read necessarily focuses your mind on what you are reading, because it is undoubtedly possible to take notes in the absence of any cerebral activity. However, note taking can be helpful in focusing your attention, provided that you become and remain conscious of your purposes as you read.

### Note taking as a way of focusing on content

Making notes can help you to learn and absorb information, when it involves making decisions about what are the main ideas in texts. However, focusing your attention in this way takes skill and must be practised, because poor note-taking habits can make it more difficult to learn.

Some students (and we hope that you are not one of these) will take copious notes whenever they read. Often such a student will virtually copy out the text he is reading and as a result he will end up with pages and pages of laboriously copied text. This can give the impression both to himself and to others that he has done lots of work. And of course he has; he has copied out lots of text. But has he used his precious time as wisely as he might have done? That is more questionable. Copying down lumps of text from books, articles, or web pages will most often have little effect on what you know and understand.

To be as beneficial as possible, note taking will have to exercise your brain. It is the exercise of thoughtful discrimination and selection – in deciding what you should write down, and of creativity – in deciding how best to write it down, that will make your note taking have a real impact on your learning and thinking. That is why you should ensure that your note taking suits your purposes.

When you are listening to a lecture, note taking can get in the way of learning – because unless you are thoughtful in doing so, taking notes can become more important than listening to what is said.

Do you recognize this scenario?

---

The lecturer has just said something like, 'So the main problem with Smith's theory, in my view, is that it fails to explain why . . .' when a student – usually one at the back who has spent the entire lecture writing furiously in his notepad – asks, 'Could you just say that again please, I missed that bit?' The lecturer, though irritated by this interruption (the fourth in this lecture so far by the same student, or one of his pals), stops and says, 'OK, what I was saying was that in my view Smith's theory doesn't seem to work because it can't explain . . .' when the student interjects, 'No, not that bit, the bit that began, 'So the main problem with Smith's theory . . .'

The problem in this story is that the student isn't listening to what the lecturer is saying, but merely copying it down, and thus fails to appreciate that, when she repeats herself, she is saying the same thing, even though the words she is using are slightly different. It is almost as if, in fact it is exactly as if, he believes that it is the particular words that the lecturer utters, rather than the ideas she is attempting to communicate, that are important.

Note taking in lectures, of the kind we are criticizing, shows an unsophisticated approach to knowledge acquisition. It has an exact parallel in the way in which some students take notes when they are reading, which focuses on the attempt to write down every detail of what the author has written. It never makes sense to take voluminous notes that are hardly shorter than the original document. All you need to note down is sufficient to remind you about:

- what the author says
- what you think about what the author says
- what, if anything, you should do to follow up your reading.

## Note taking as interrogation

Knowing what you would like to gain from reading a text will help you to interrogate it in a way that gives you the best chance of gaining as much as possible from the relationship you develop with it. The same approach is also useful when you come to take notes about texts, especially when you are trying to come to terms with or uncover the reasoning an author has followed.

One of us, who only ever takes notes when he wants to read a text in detail, always undertakes such reading while sitting in front of a computer, in order that he can take notes as he reads, working directly on to screen. As he reads, he records what he thinks the author is saying. In addition, when appropriate, he records what he thinks about what the author is saying, and also the response he would expect the author to give to his comments. He raises (for himself, because the author, of course, is not present to offer a defence) objections to the author's line of reasoning or arguments, noting points where he needs more information. He also records any new ideas he has as a result of reading what the author has written. In this way, he proceeds through the text, line by line, sentence by sentence, paragraph by paragraph, in a dialogue with the author. Consider, for example, the notes that follow, which one of us made in relation to a single paragraph of text while reading Florence Nightingale's *Notes on Nursing*, first published in 1859:

**Music.** The effect of music upon the sick has been scarcely at all noticed. In fact, its expensiveness, as it is now, makes any general application of it quite out of the question. I will only remark here, that wind instruments, including the human voice, and stringed instruments, capable of continuous sound, have a generally beneficent effect – while the piano-forte, with such instruments as have *no* continuity of sound, has just the reverse. The finest piano-forte playing will damage the sick, while an air, like 'Home, sweet home', or 'Assisa a pie d'un salice', on the most ordinary grinding organ will sensibly soothe them – and this quite independent of association. Florence Nightingale, *Notes on Nursing* (1980 edition, p.44).

**Music.** The effect of music upon the sick has been scarcely at all noticed.

HAS WORK BEEN DONE ON THE THERAPEUTIC EFFECTS OF MUSIC ON PHYSICALLY ILL PEOPLE – IF IT HAD, WOULD THEY STILL DO PIPED RUBBISH MUSIC THROUGH THE HEADPHONES IN NHS HOSPITALS?

In fact, its expensiveness, as it is now, makes any general application of it quite out of the question.

NOT SO EXPENSIVE NOW FLO! SHE GOES ON TO SAY THAT WIND INSTRUMENTS (IN WHICH SHE INCLUDES THE HUMAN VOICE) AND STRINGED INSTRUMENTS, WHICH ARE

capable of continuous sound, have generally a beneficent effect.

HOWEVER, SHE DOESN'T SEEM TO LIKE PIANOS

the finest piano-forte music will damage the sick

I WONDER WHAT SHE'D THINK OF POP MUSIC AND MORE *PARTICULARLY OF PIPED MUSIC?* TO WHAT EXTENT WOULD WHAT WAS THERAPEUTIC VARY BETWEEN PEOPLE – DEPENDING, FOR EXAMPLE, ON PERSONAL TASTE? IS THERE ANY MUSIC THAT WOULD BE GOOD FOR EVERYONE? I GUESS SOME MUSIC MIGHT BE GOOD FOR PEOPLE, EVEN IF THEY DIDN'T LIKE IT. HAVE CONTROLLED TRIALS BEEN DONE ON THIS? WOULD THEY BE ETHICAL?

This form of note taking is time consuming but rewarding. It can be useful as a way of approaching text that you want to read very carefully. If you adopt it you will often find that by the time you reach the end of a passage you know something you did not know before, or that you understand something that previously you could not fathom.

Best of all, if you engage in this detailed approach to reading and note taking – moving between the attempt to understand and the attempt to respond – you will find that it often results in text that, after refashioning and elaborating, can be used in your essays. Treated in this painstaking way, the apparently simple task of taking notes can thus be viewed as an opportunity to develop your own ideas and text. However, a word of caution is called for. In order to avoid the possibility of inadvertently plagiarizing authors, which could result in severe penalties including expulsion from your course, you must make sure that whenever you engage with texts in this detailed and painstaking way, you clearly distinguish their words – and their ideas – from your own. In the example above this was achieved by using upper case letters for commentary, and lower case letters for Florence Nightingale's words.

## SOME IMPORTANT ADVICE

### Don't allow yourself to be persuaded to take notes in a way that doesn't suit you

It is important that the form of note taking that you use in recording your reading suits you and helps you to record, remember, and use information. There is absolutely no good in working out which key words best sum up a text if, later, you have no idea at all what those key words mean. Equally, there is no point in drawing elaborate web diagrams, showing all sorts of relationships between ideas, if you cannot use them later in constructing an adequate view or critique of what an author said. And the fact that your best friend (who is a really good note taker) uses coloured pens to transcribe notes of different kinds (red for facts, green for opinions, blue for arguments, black for examples, say) should not induce you to follow suit, if the use of colours just confuses you.

**Promiscuity in note taking is OK**

Don't allow yourself to fall into the trap of believing that you are the kind of person who takes notes in one prescribed way. Mixing and matching in note taking is OK. Sometimes the best way of recording the work you have done on a text might be to write straightforward linear notes, while at others a diagram might be more appropriate; and sometimes each will be appropriate in relation to different aspects of the same text. Even if you settle down as a note taker of a particular kind, at times you may find it worthwhile to take a holiday from your habitual approach. Every so often, try writing some notes in a style that is foreign to you. Doing this may help you to avoid stagnation and you may even find that this style is more attractive to you now than it used to be. For example, if you normally take linear notes, try making a diagram to show what you have learned from an article you have read; and if you normally make diagrams, try, occasionally, taking notes of a linear kind. Alternatively, you might want to take some existing notes about a text and try rewriting them in a different style.

## SUMMARIZING TEXTS: PARAPHRASE OR PRECIS?

A useful way of limbering up for note taking can be to practise reading passages for their essence – for the bare bones of their meaning – with a view to rendering them into a shorter form. The ability to extract the essence of a text involves two skills – paraphrase and precis – which, though distinct, are often confused. Both can be helpful in nurturing your ability to read texts carefully, because they demand that you develop the ability to spot what is essential.

To paraphrase a piece of text is to put it into your own words. You will find skill in paraphrasing useful when you want to give an account of an author's views, before going on to critique them or to compare them with others. However, you should make sure that you do not use such skill to allow you to pass off as your own, ideas from others; to do so is plagiarism, just as much as stealing their words.

Probably even more useful than skill in paraphrasing are the skills needed to precis a passage. A precis is a summary – a shorter version – of a text, which nonetheless contains all the main points. Whereas in paraphrase the attempt is made to render text into your own words, precis usually involves using the author's words, except where another formulation would allow significant shortening. Though there is no formulaic way of undertaking a precis, you should take note of these suggestions.

---

### Points to bear in mind when constructing a precis

Don't start your precis till you are sure you have grasped the main points in the text.

Try to use the author's words unless significant savings are to be made by recasting what is said in other words; never change the author's meaning.

Spot key words and use them.

Use as few words to render each sentence, phrase and paragraph as will allow you to retain the intended sense.

Never say things more than once, even if the original does.

Remove anything that is inessential – that is merely 'decorative' or interesting. Depending on the required length, this may involve removing examples and illustrations which are secondary to the main thread.

Reduce the number of adjectives and adverbs to a minimum.

Make sure your precis is grammatically correct and is spelled and punctuated correctly.

---

We want you now to undertake a little practice in precis, first in relation to a couple of passages written by others, and then in relation to something you have written yourself.

| Practising precis | Task 6.8 |

Read the following brief passage which offers an overview of some of the central features of a philosophical position known as 'idealism'. Then precis it in as few words as possible.

Idealism, in its various forms, shares the common belief that the so-called 'external world' is somehow created by the mind. Physical objects are viewed as existing only in relation to an experiencing subject, so that reality is conceived of in terms of mind or experience. Idealism, in its full-blooded form, holds that reality is mental and that matter does not exist except as ideas in the mind – the individual mind, minds in general, or the mind of God. It holds that our senses inform us about ideas but not about material substances to which those ideas belong.

(Poole, M. (1995) *Beliefs and Values in Science Education*, p.45)

In attempting to precis Poole's passage, one of us went through the following steps in thinking about what is more and less essential to its meaning.

i *Idealism, in its various forms* . . . 'in its various forms' tells us that there is more than one kind of idealism, but since this is a side issue, we could easily omit it in a slimmed down version.

ii *shares the common belief that the so-called 'external world' is somehow created by the mind* . . . 'common'; 'so-called' and 'somehow' do little real work, and so we can omit them.

iii *Physical objects are viewed as existing only in relation to an experiencing subject* . . . and . . . *so that reality is conceived of in terms of mind or experience* . . . say very similar things and might be condensed as, for example, 'Physical objects are conceived of in terms of mind or experience'.

iv *Idealism, in its full-blooded form* . . . implies that what follows is the essence of idealism; however, in a slimmed down version we could probably dispense with 'in its full-blooded form'.

v *holds that reality is mental and that matter does not exist
except as ideas in the mind – the individual mind, minds in
general, or the mind of God* . . . the main thing here is the
idea that reality is mental and that matter only exists as
ideas in the mind. We can thus dispense with the statement of the various possible minds in which they might
exist. In addition 'holds that reality is mental' repeats
what was said earlier about external reality being created
by the mind, and can be omitted.

vi *It holds that our senses inform us about ideas but not about
material substances to which those ideas belong.* We can safely
omit 'It holds'.

Following these steps results in a precis which captures most of
the main points.

Idealism is the belief that the 'external world' is created by
the mind; physical objects are conceived of in terms of mind
or experience. It holds that matter does not exist except as
ideas in the mind, that our senses inform us about ideas but
not about material substances.

Precis involves not only skill but judgement, understanding and
knowledge. Each person who attempts to precis a passage will
thus produce a different version, because they will each weigh
up and prioritize its elements differently. We thought it might be
interesting to illustrate this by having a number of people precis
the same passage and so not only did we both attempt to precis
the passage about idealism, we also asked our children do so;
finally we invited Mary West, their 95-year-old nana, to do so.
Gavin's precis is given above; the others are as follows:

Idealism is the belief that the external world is created by the
mind. Reality and matter are non-existent except as ideas in
the mind of individuals, populations or God. Senses do not
inform us about material substances but about related ideas.

(Susan)

One view of idealism is that reality does not exist except in
the mind by which the external world is created. Our senses
inform us about ideas, but not about material objects which
exist only through experience.

(Thomas)

Idealism has the belief that the external world is all in the mind. Physical objects are seen as only being in relation to an experiencing subject, so reality is conceived *in* minds or experience. Idealism in its full-blooded form, holds that reality is mental, and that matter does not exist only as ideas in our minds, or in the mind of God. So our senses give us ideas, but do not tell us about material substances which formed the ideas.

(Mary)

Idealism believes that the external world is made by the mind. Objects are viewed as existing to an experiencing subject, so reality is thought of in terms of mind or experience. Idealism in its strongest form, holds reality is mental and doesn't exist except in the mind – the individual mind or the mind of God. It holds that our senses tell us about ideas but not material substances to which those ideas belong.

(Faith)

How does your precis compare with these five attempts to precis the same passage? Is it more or less accurate in summing up the original passage? Is it longer or shorter? Does it cover all the same details?

Precis is such a useful skill that it is worth taking the time to practise it and we suggest that you should try to do so. Obviously it is best if you do this in relation to texts from your own subject. However, there is something to be said, also, for practising precis in relation to texts from other academic areas.

Practising precis is a good way of developing your skills as an academic reader and note taker. It will also assist your development as an academic writer. You need not choose long passages – a paragraph or two will be sufficient. Nor need you always take the time to make your own rendition as good as it might be. However, it is worthwhile trying to get as much practice as you can in understanding passages as thoroughly as possible, and in rendering the sense of what authors wish to convey as clearly and simply and as economically as possible.

## Precising your own work

Skill in precis can come in handy not only when you are attempting to get to grips with a text written by someone else, but in relation to your own work. Professional authors are only too aware of the strict word limits that are often laid down by, for example, academic journals, and skill in precis can help them to reduce an article down from its original length to that required for the journal of their choice. Although it is often hard to excise one's own words (they are after all rather like one's babies), cutting down an article in this way often leads to better, crisper and cleaner prose.

---

| **Write a precis of one of your own essays** | *Task 6.9* |

Look out one of your old essays. Then, working either with the whole text or with a discrete section, count the number of words it contains, decide on the number of words you will allow yourself for a precis and then get stuck in. You might decide to go through a number of stages – beginning, say, by cutting the essay down by a third of the original number of words, then reducing the number even further.

---

In writing your precis, did you bear in mind all the points that we list on page 118? We devote the whole of Part 10 to a discussion of the importance of reading your own work. This is one of the most important areas in which, as a student, you will have to develop skills and, perhaps even more importantly, discipline. Attempting, from time to time, to precis your own work is a good way of developing ability in reading it closely.

**And finally . . .**

---

| **And finally . . . two more passages to precis** | *Task 6.10* |

Before moving on to Part 7, which focuses on the ways in which reading and writing are related, we would like you to practise writing precis of a couple of contrasting passages. The first is taken from a philosophical discussion of biomedical ethics, and the second from a psychological book about depression.

**Passage from Maclean, A. (1993)** *The Elimination of Morality: Reflections on Utilitarianism and Bioethics.* **London: Routledge, pp.5–6.**

The objection I wish to make to the bioethical enterprise is a fundamental one. It is that philosophy as such delivers no verdict upon moral issues; there is no unique set of moral principles which philosophy as such underwrites and no question, therefore, of using that set to uncover the answers which philosophy gives to moral questions. When bioethicists deliver a verdict upon the moral issues raised by medical practice, it is their own verdict they deliver and not the verdict of philosophy itself; it is their voice we hear and not the voice of reason or rationality. To say this, it must be emphasised, is not to deny that there can be rational answers to moral questions; it is to deny that, for any moral question, there is a *uniquely* rational answer to it which can be uncovered by philosophical enquiry. My claim is not that rational justification is impossible in morality, but that it is not the sort of thing bioethicists say it is. It is their conception of rational justification I wish to reject and not the concept itself.

Consider the bioethicist's attitude to *moral disagreements.* I said above that bioethicists regard such disagreements as bad things, things we must strive to eradicate. When people disagree about a moral question raised by medical practice, the business of medical ethics, according to bioethicists, is to settle this disagreement by resolving the matter at issue – by discerning which of the competing views, if any, is the rationally justified view. It is not possible, in their eyes, for both of two opposing moral judgements or points of view to have a rational justification; if one is rationally justified, they think, *really* rationally justified, then the other cannot be. Where disagreement exists, the views of one (at least) of the parties to the disagreement must be defective from the standpoint of reason or rationality.

**Passage from Rowe, D. (1983)** *Depression: The Way Out of your Prison.* **London: Routledge and Kegan Paul, pp.52–3.**

... There was a time when you thought that if you turned your back on the past and ran as fast as you could the future would open up, rosy with promise. However, once inside the prison of depression you know that running on a treadmill makes no progress, that there is nowhere to progress to, and all you are left with is a past which is filled with fear, anger, jealousy, regret, grief and loss.

The famous French psychiatrist, Henri Ey, considered that the most important feature of depression was the way in which the person's perception of time changed, not just the slowing down of time so that twenty-four hours passed like a week, but the relative importance of past and future, so that the past and not the future engages the depressed person's attention. It is not the kind of interest in the past that many people develop as they approach old age, when they spend a lot of time thinking about past events and telling their stories to every willing and unwilling listener available. Usually the story is told in the framework of 'things were better then than they are now', even when the events re-called involved suffering and hardship, since the person is in the business of showing that he had not been conquered and defeated, but that he had mastered life and enjoyed it, and, since the con-temporary world is inferior to that of his youth, nothing is to be gained by living for ever. In such a way do elderly people become reconciled to their lives and so reconciled to their deaths. They recall their past to redefine it as good.

But your living in the past is quite different. When you do recall something that was good and happy, you do this not with pleas-ure but with painful regret. Something, or somebody, has been lost, never to return. When you see this loss as having occurred not by chance but by carelessness or malice, your memories are filled by bitterness, anger and resentment. You have suffered many losses, rebuffs, unsettling changes, some of which would be categ-orised by sociologists as the 'life events' which depressed people, so research shows, collect in greater numbers than non-depressed people (you always knew you were unlucky!) and some of which were the small betrayals, deceits, disloyalties, treacheries, cruelties, dishonesties, denunciations, threats, belittlings, rejections, criticisms, reproaches, indignities, jealousies, animosities, ingratitudes, mean-nesses, enmities and ostracisms that take place in every community which is not guided by love and forgiveness.

# PART 7: Reading and writing

There's a line in an old song that goes, 'Love and marriage, love and marriage, go together like a horse and carriage' (Cahn 1955). Reading and writing are like that – they go together, even if it would be quaintly old fashioned of us to believe this of love and marriage nowadays. Or at least they should go together when you are writing as an academic – both now, as a student, and later, if you make a career in research or teaching. Your reading should inform your writing and your needs as a writer should underpin much of what you read. In Part 7 we address the relationship between what you read and what you write, as a student.

## READING AND WRITING: TWO SIDES OF THE SAME COIN?

You have been a writer for as long as you have been a reader and, like many students, you may have reasons for believing that you are quite skilled – an 'A' in A level English? A mum who really liked your stories when you were in primary school? Good marks for most of your written work? Kind and congratulatory comments on essays you have written – 'Good work. You are beginning to develop your own voice; keep it up!' – that kind of thing. If you are not living with the benefits of such adulation, you may be ready for the advice we have to give you. We hope so, because it is important, if you are to be as successful as you can be as a student, that you should learn to write as well as possible. Even if you have good reasons for believing in your ability to write, however, we hope that you do not let them go to your head, and that you will be willing to think seriously about what we have to say.

Throughout the book we have suggested that in reading academic texts you should always make the attempt to engage with their authors, relating what they have written to what you already know, interrogating them via their text. When you are reading as a student you will often be reading with the intention of gathering information to use in your written work. In other words, your reading and writing will be closely linked, like two sides of the same coin.

The ways in which you read will (or at least should) be influenced by what you need to find out in order to answer the questions you have been set; they will also depend upon the level of understanding you need in order to be able to utilize those texts in your written work.

The ways in which you speak are influenced by the ways in which you hear other people speaking – your family; the people you meet at school or university; and public figures, including politicians and those who interview them on television and radio. Similarly, the ways in which you write will be influenced (whether you are aware of it or not) by authors you read. You will be influenced by the way they use words and by the words they use, by their use of punctuation and by the ways in which they structure their arguments and present their points of view. Unfortunately, this will not necessarily be a good thing, because some academic authors write very poorly and it is important to beware of falling into the trap of believing that, just because many academic authors write in impenetrable, incoherent and jargon-laden prose, this is the way that you should write. In order to ensure that your writing is influenced positively by the things you read, you will thus have to read other authors carefully, taking note of the ways in which they express themselves –

what works and does not work in their writing. Doing this will allow you to improve your written work by emulating the effect-ive elements of their style, while avoiding at least some of its pitfalls.

Your reading will, even more obviously, influence what you write about. As a student you will be expected to demonstrate that you are familiar with at least some of what has been written about your subject. In addition to giving those who read your work details about sources from which you have gathered factual information, this will allow you to make use of what other authors have written, in building your own point of view or argument. You will be able to do this regardless of whether you agree with the authors of texts, or consider that they have argued well. In order to do so, you will have to adopt common conventions of academic *citation* and *referencing*. Whenever you refer to an author's ideas in your written work, you will have to make clear that you are doing so by *citing* her in your text; you will also have to give a full *reference* to her work, which will usually appear in a list at the end of your assignment. That is why we want to give you guidance about the *Harvard* system for academic citation and referencing. Before doing so, however, we want to talk about some of the ways in which your reading might influence your writing.

### Using your reading to develop your text

When you are reading, you will have to make decisions about whether the points of view and arguments that authors present, the evidence to which they point, and the examples they utilize, are worth using to support the development of your own argu-ments and points of view, and, if so, how best to use them.

There are many hazards you must avoid if you are to become a writer able to make use of your reading in developing both the text of your assignments and the arguments they contain. Among the most common of these, at least among novice academic writers, is the danger of falling into the trap of always citing authors as if what they say is true, even when it may be in considerable doubt. Another trap is that of thinking that because an author's view-point coincides with your own, it will necessarily enhance your case if you mention in your essay that this author shares your view, or some part of it.

Students fall into these traps more often when they first enter higher education. However, they sometimes continue to do so for a long time unless they are helped, by their teachers, to realize that part of what is expected of them is that they should develop critical skill, and the ability to make reasoned decisions about the credibility of the things that they read. Throughout this book we emphasize again and again the need to reflect critically on what authors say. Whenever you use another person's reasoning to support your own viewpoint, you should always try to give cogent reasons for doing so.

In deciding whether to use an author's arguments in your essay, you will have to be able to unpick them, tracking them through the texts you are reading. This is not an easy business. Academic authors are sometimes less than clear in the arguments they put forward. Even when they are clear, their lines of thought are often very complex, with many side tracks and trails, and so many illustrative examples that, as a reader, you may find your-self wondering how on earth you got to the point you have reached in the text, and where the argument is going next. You would be well advised to seek some help in developing the skills necessary to track and understand arguments well enough to allow you to assess whether or not they are good arguments. There are a number of texts in print that might help you to do so, including *Critical Reasoning* (Thomson 1996); *Thinking – A to Z* (Warburton 1996); and *How to Think Straight* (Flew 1998), as well as the third part of *Reading, Writing and Reasoning* (Fairbairn and Winch 1996).

## *The patchwork approach*

A surprisingly large number of students, even in the second and third year of a degree course, adopt a simplistic approach to using the things they have learned from their reading, which involves merely harvesting ideas from authors who have ad-dressed their topic and merging them in a kind of Frankenstein's monster of an essay. Such essays are comprised of a mixture of direct quotations and sections of work by others, subtly (and sometimes not so subtly) paraphrased into their 'own words'.

Often, in such an essay, there is little to suggest that an author was present at its creation, because there is little evidence of a developed viewpoint, rather than an account of what others think. Since the views that are being put forward do not belong to the student but to others, this approach is in some ways a safe way to proceed. After all, you cannot be criticized for your point of view, if you do not present it. Of course, neither can you be praised or given credit for your view, if you fail to reveal it. As a result, if your tutor is awake when she reads it, you are unlikely to gain high marks for an essay of this kind, because such work usually demonstrates little critical ability and will often fail even to demonstrate understanding of the topic.

### Use what you have read as scaffolding on which to build your case

A better, though more scary, way to use your reading is to employ the things you have read as scaffolding to support your own arguments and points of view. In this case, though you must be careful to ensure that your accounts of others are accurate, what really matters is the views you use them to support. This approach involves more critical judgement because, to switch metaphors for a moment, it involves both 'setting out your stall' – that is, making clear what you believe – and making decisions about which evidence, from authors you have read, can be put to best use in supporting your own developing points of view.

### Demonstrate your ability to think critically

Finally, you can use the work you have done in reading round your topic to demonstrate your ability to think critically about what others have said. This will involve doing more than simply showing that you understand ideas and arguments and evidence in what others have written that support or help to form your own point of view. In addition, you will have to show that you are able to pinpoint flaws in their reasoning. Academic reading is always a critical pursuit, in the sense that it involves interrogating the author via her text, assessing what she writes for coherence and clarity as well as for the strength of her arguments and for the relevance and strength of the examples, illustrations and evidence she uses. Reading in this way helps us to build our knowledge and understanding; it helps to form our interests in research and scholarship at the same time as developing our own views and the arguments that are necessary to support them. It is a crucial part of the process of academic writing, whether at undergraduate, postgraduate or professional level.

When you come across arguments that support your own point of view, or that help to shape it, you will be able to cite them directly in support of your own position. However, rather than simply pointing out that other people share your view, or part of it, you should always give reasons for accepting their arguments. The fact that someone else, however eminent, agrees with your position is never a reason for blindly accepting what they say as evidence in your favour; you must always make the attempt to show why their position is attractive and their arguments strong.

You may decide that though it is, or seems to be, mistaken, an argument that an author presents is still worth discussing in building up your own point of view. Demonstrating what is mistaken about opposing points of view can be useful in helping to persuade others of the attractiveness of your own position. However, it is important to realize that, whether you agree with them or not, you should always try to be respectful of the authors whose work you read, even when you think they are making mistakes. This is true even if the mistakes they have made seem fatal to their argument.

If you want to make use of a point of view that an author has put forward, that you believe to be mistaken, it is especially important to treat what they say respectfully, since you are likely to make even more impact if, before presenting your critique, you state the author's position or argument as fairly and as accurately as possible. Doing so will make your view all the more powerful, because it demonstrates mastery of the position you intend to attack, and thus strengthens your claim to be able to pinpoint its weaknesses. After presenting the argument or position you wish to attack as sympathetically as you can, showing how the various steps follow from one another, and contribute (or are thought by the author to contribute) to the conclusion reached, you should point out flaws in the author's line of reasoning, drawing attention to places where the various steps do not follow from one another and, perhaps, to mistakes in facts or understanding that lead you to reject it. You will then be able to show how your position overcomes or helps to overcome the problems you have noted. This is a more sophisticated use of citation, but one that is likely to gain you brownie points. As you read, you should thus note weaknesses in the arguments that authors present, and consider whether and how they might be made stronger.

Less obvious, perhaps, is the idea of making use of flawed arguments offered by those whose conclusions mirror your own, or whose conclusions you find attractive and would want to defend. In this case uncovering a weakness can allow you to show that you are willing to be critical of those who share your views as well as of those who oppose them.

## CITATION AND REFERENCING: THE PRACTICALITIES

We turn now to a discussion of the practicalities of citation and referencing. Citing others in your written work should give those who read your essay the opportunity to follow up your references for themselves, and to check that you are accurate in what you have said. And so, whether or not you choose to adopt our suggestions, it is important that you are consistent and clear in the conventions you adopt, making sure that you give sufficient information about all cited sources to allow readers to locate them, if they wish to do so.

### How much reference to what you have read should you make in your essays?

In Part 3 we talked about how surprised one of us was in his previous job to discover that colleagues, who should have known better, were telling students how many references they were expected to cite in their essays; it is almost as if those who act like this believe that the number of references a person uses when he writes can somehow allow readers to make an assessment of what he knows (and that the more he cites, the better).

We disagree wholeheartedly with this belief. Nonetheless, since your lecturers may embrace it, you will have to decide for yourself how you should act.

In our view, you should avoid using citation to give public displays either of how clever you are, or of how much you have read; doing so can lead to bad reading habits, including the habit of directing your reading towards the collection of 'trophies' that you can use to decorate your essays, rather than engaging with the ideas that authors are attempting to convey, or the arguments that they are attempting to present.

---

**When should you cite?**

Only cite references where, for example:

- they are necessary to show that you have evidence for what you are saying
- you want to acknowledge that ideas you are using have come from other people
- in building your argument or viewpoint, you wish to criticize another person's views or arguments.

Never cite others simply to give the impression that you have read something but only to show how you have been influenced by what you have read.

---

## To quote or not to quote?

Some students, especially but not exclusively in the early part of their career as students, develop the misguided idea that whenever they refer to an author's work they must directly quote something that she says. Even students who claim to understand that there is more to citation than this often give a direct quotation on most, if not all, occasions, when they refer to the work of others.

Directly quoting an author's words can be useful. However, as a general rule, you should not quote another person's words directly unless you have good reason for doing so. For example, you might quote an author because:

- she has managed to say what you want to say more clearly, more elegantly and more economically than you could say it
- it is important, for the purposes of your argument, that you give the exact words, for example, if you wish to criticize what she has written
- the words you are citing are from a literary source such as a novel, poem, play or film script. This is a distinctive use of quotation, and it is clearly different from occasions when you are citing a person in developing an argument.

If you do find it necessary to quote directly from another person, you should ensure that you are accurate in your quotation, always taking it directly from the cited source. You should be as brief as possible (in most instances more than 50 words is likely to be longer than necessary). In addition you must make clear why you are doing so. Quotes should never be used merely for decorative purposes, or as a way of showing that you have read something. Quotations that suddenly appear in the middle of a piece of text like decorations on a Christmas tree, without any explanation as to why they are there, are not useful. 'Ornament cannot disguise the lack of wholeness in the inner life of man' (James 1947). Quotations should always be introduced. Did you notice how the quotation from James (an invented author by the way) suddenly appeared with no warning?

### How to introduce quotations?

There is no general rule about how to introduce quotations. However, short quotations are usually indicated by the use of speech marks ('Like this'), while longer ones are usually set off from the main body of text in a separate paragraph, without the use of speech marks. In addition to citing the author, and the year in which the work was published, in your text, you should give the page number/s on which the words quoted appear.

*Example 1*
Beauchamp and Childress (1983), whose views of the nature of suicide are somewhat simplistic, believe that where a person who is dying of a terminal illness allows himself to die, '. . . we are reluctant to call the act suicide' (p.93).

*Example 2*

Attacking the tendency among psychologists to detach themselves from their subjects Mair (1970) writes:

> When I hear people accuse psychologists of being isol-
> ated from the real world, small minded, hidebound by
> doctrine and method, incapable of learning from experi-
> ence, I have to laugh. After all, I know, personally, half
> a dozen (well at least three) psychologists who, after
> only a few years of dedicated experimentation in their
> discipline, and despite very expensive and lengthy train-
> ing to the contrary, have been forced to change some of
> their fundamental professional beliefs and accept that
> the subjects they have been herding through their labor-
> atories *are human* after all. (p.1)

## Two systems of citation and referencing

While you are reading, you will come across different ways of
citing academic references and other work. Those that you are
most likely to encounter as you read are:

- the 'Harvard system' (also known as the 'author–date
  system')
- the 'numeric system'.

Since this is a book about reading rather than writing, we do
not intend to go into a detailed discussion of the whole range of
citation systems (there are, for example, a number of variations
on the 'author–date' system, which go by different names). We
will briefly introduce you to the Harvard system, because it is
very common, easy to learn, and will allow you to be accurate in
your use of citation and referencing. After that we will say a little
about the numerical system, because you will probably read books
and articles which use it.

## Using the Harvard system

The Harvard system involves two things:

i  citation within the text
ii the provision of a full bibliographical reference.

You may notice slight differences between the way we suggest that you should cite sources using the Harvard system, and the way in which our own citations are given in this book. Similarly, you may well spot deviations between the ways in which we suggest that you should present information about sources in a reference list, and the ways in which references are presented in the reference list at the end of the book (pp.202–3). Please do not allow yourself to be alarmed about this. Though we suggest commonly adopted forms for citation and referencing, you will undoubtedly come across a range of different ways of presenting such information, and you may find that you are required to adopt a different system for the purposes of your assignments, just as we have had to modify our presentation in order to fit in with Open University Press house style. What is important is that you give full and accurate information and that you are consistent in the ways in which you do so.

### Citation within the text

Whenever you refer to an author, you should insert the date of publication in brackets after her name. For example, if you were referring to an article by Barker, which was published in 1998, you might write, 'Barker (1998) argues . . .', or 'By contrast, Barker (1998) holds the view that . . .'. Our view (and it is by no means universally shared) is that citation is always best when authors make the effort to include the names of those to whom they wish to refer, in their text, as in the examples about Barker. Doing so makes it easier to be clear about why the person in question is being cited. However, you may find yourself drawn to a rather more common and, in our view, less helpful mode of citation, in which the reader is left to guess at the reason that an author is being cited. In this style of citation, the author's name and the date of publication are given in brackets at the appropriate point in your text. For example, you might write, 'There is a great deal of disagreement about the best way of approaching this disputed area of practice (Smith 1987; MacMinn 1998). Notice that we have no way of telling which side of the fence Smith and MacMinn sit on, from this citation.

However you choose to cite authors within your text, you should ensure that it is clear when you are using ideas from others. This means that you may at times have to cite the same author and the same source several times. However, you need not give the reference repeatedly where you continue to talk about the same author for a paragraph or so, provided that it remains obvious who you are talking about.

Where you are referring to a source that has more than one author, you will probably want to use all of their names in referring to them if this does not interfere with the flow of your essay. However, where there are more than two or three authors, the abbreviation 'et al.' is often used to indicate 'this author and others'. Where you refer to sources published in the same year by the same author(s), you should distinguish them using lower case letters. In general, you should only use family names in citation – unless, for example, you are referring to two Smiths, when you might use the initials of their first names to distinguish them in the text of your essay.

In general, you should not give the title of sources in your text; doing so uses up valuable words and may make your text cluttered and more difficult to follow. One exception to this might be where you are citing a classic work, such as Charles Darwin's *The Origin of Species*. Others might be where to do so adds something to the text or where, for example in a literature essay, you are referring to a work of art such as a novel, play or poem rather than to an academic text.

In general, you do not have to give page references within your text unless you are quoting directly from another person (see our discussion of direct quotation on pages 132–4). However, you may choose to do so if, for example, you are referring to different parts of a large document, or the text to which you are referring is long and/or complex so that the idea to which you are referring may be difficult to locate.

Textual references in the Harvard style can take many forms. For example,

Tomkins (2000) has recently suggested that the use of paper based literary technology will soon be a thing of the past.

Recent studies argue that characteristic behaviours of advanced primates such as chimpanzees and gorillas provide evidence of a rudimentary kind of morality (see, for example, Thomas 1972; Radley and Jenkins 1981; Fischer 1987).

In a seminal article Donaldson (1967) argued that cats have no linguistic ability. Later, reporting on extensive research with a particularly brainy cat called Tiddles (Donaldson 1977a), he argued that if Tiddles couldn't be taught to talk, then it was unlikely that any cat would ever develop linguistic ability. However, he soon revised this view (Donaldson 1977b).

One way of doing this would be to adapt an approach that Mead and I have used in working on moral issues with nursing students (Fairbairn and Mead 1990, 1992a, 1992b).

In a recent groundbreaking article Murray and Taylor (1999) related the processes involved in making a decent cup of coffee without either coffee beans or water to some of the most fundamental problems of both theology and physics.

A recent study (Bailey et al. 1988) described the incidence of premature greyness among college lecturers and argued that it usually results from traumatic encounters with illiterate students.

Recent and important developments in thinking about the teaching of English in schools have been given a public airing through a number of official documents. (See, for example, *English in the National Curriculum*, DES, Welsh Office 1990).

In this classic study, Draycott (1924, p.196) argued that history always repeats itself.

### What if you cannot gain access to a source to which another author has referred?

When in the course of your reading you come across interesting references to other work, you will probably want to look them up yourself. This is especially important if you want to refer to them in your work. However, it will sometimes be impossible to do so. For example, the relevant journal or book may not be held by your library or it may be so popular that you cannot get access to it in time. In such a case, if inter-library loan is out of the question and you still wish to make reference to the source cited by others, you should cite, and give a full reference to, the author whose work you have actually read, rather than to the person or persons they in turn are citing. For example, you might write:

> Tompkins (1993) reports research by Wilson (1986) suggesting that schools which have a uniform tend to achieve more success in public examinations than those that do not.

> Campbell and Collinson (1988, p.19) cite Harada who writes, 'It was not mere suicide. It was an institution, legal and ceremonial . . . by which warriors could expiate their friends or prove their sincerity.'

### Problems with the Harvard system for citation

For all its convenience and ease of use, the Harvard system can disrupt the flow of the text and, in order to facilitate the communication of your ideas, you should avoid using more references than necessary. Do not throw in textual references just to show off how much you have read (or are aware of); it is difficult to avoid the suspicion that those who over-reference are not fully familiar with many of the sources they cite. Try to avoid this kind of thing which is prevalent in some areas of academic writing:

> Many of the recent changes to the National Health Service have caused major disruption (Atherton, Radcliffe and Riley 1988; Barlow 1977; Bolton Hwang and Beer 1991; de Pear 1987; Dobson 1987, 1988a, 1991; Doverner 1992b; Francey 1986; Langley and Smith 1987; Maclean and Burrows 1987; MacMinn 1975; Scrimshaw 1995c; Thomson et al. 1991; Wilton 1992, 1993). Given this fact, it is hardly surprising to find a certain amount of discontent among the workforce.

Over-referencing will be especially irritating for those who read your work if you are unclear about your reasons for citation. For example, we do not know whether the authors cited above simply raise the point about major disruption having been caused. Do they simply assert this claim? Or do they give examples to support it? Perhaps they even dispute this idea.

## *Location and arrangement of bibliographical reference lists*

The information you should provide in bibliographical references will depend on the source you are citing, for example whether it is a book, an article, or an electronic source. Not only that, but there is considerable variation in the ways in which different people, including publishers, arrange such information. However, the following examples illustrate some commonly accepted ways of giving most kinds of source, except those relating to electronic sources, where an accepted form of referencing is yet to emerge; however, we do include examples of possible ways of presenting information about some such sources. Notice that the way in which you should punctuate (and even the order of the elements that make up references) is not laid down in stone, and you will thus come across authors who do things differently than us; you may even be instructed or advised to do things differently. What is important is that the information should allow your readers to locate the material you cite. References should be arranged in an alphabetical list at the end of the text.

Almond, B. (1988) *Philosophy*, London, Penguin.

Arret, W. 'Nine Planets – Comets', April 2, 1997 http://seds. Lpl.arizona.edu/nineplanets/nineplanets/comets.html

Arras, J. (1997) 'Nice Story, But So What? Narrative and Justification in Ethics' in Lindemann Nelson, H. (ed) *Stories and their Limits: Narrative Approaches to Bioethics*, New York and London, Routledge.

Bailey, M. 'Halley's Comet', *Microsoft ® Encarta ® 98 Encyclopaedia*, 1998 Edition.

Becker, E. (1980) *The Birth and Death of Meaning* (2nd Edn), Harmondsworth, Penguin.

Becker, H.S. (1968) 'The self and adult socialisation', in Norbeck, E., Price-Williams, D. and McCord, W.M. (eds) (1980) *The Study of Personality*, New York, Holt, Rinehart & Winston.

'Benjamin Disraeli' *Microsoft ® Encarta ® 98 Encyclopaedia*, 1998 Edition.

Carson, A. (carsona@newi.ac.uk) 1999. Your recent message about the new system. 23 October, email to: Gavin Fairbairn (gfairbai@glam.ac.uk)

Davis, A. (1987) 'Women with disabilities: Abortion and liberation', *Disability, Handicap and Society*, 2 (3) 275–284.

Dyer, C. (1003) 'Lords lift last bar to mercy death', *The Guardian*, 4th March, p.1.

Fairbairn, G. (1996) 'Suicide, Language and Clinical Practice', paper read at the First International Conference on *Philosophy and Psychiatry* at The Hotel Triton, Benalmadena, Spain, February.

Fairbairn, G., Rowley, D. and Bowen, M. (1995) *Sexuality, learning difficulties and doing what's right*, London, David Fulton.

'JPL   Shoemaker   –   Levy   Home   Page',   http://www.jpl.nasa.gov/sl9/image17.html

Ledermann, E.K. (1985a) *Mental Health and Human Conscience: The True and the False Self*, Aylesbury, Gower.

Ledermann, E.K. (1985b) 'Mechanism and holism in physical medicine', *Explorations in Medicine*, 1 (1).

Mead, D. (1996) Personal communication.

Orbach, S. (1980) *Fat is a Feminist Issue*, London, Hamlyn.

Orbach, S. (1984) *Fat is a Feminist Issue 2*, London, Arrow Books.

Schmidtz, D. (1998) 'Are all species equal?', *Journal of Applied Philosophy*, Vol 15, No 1, pp.57–68.

Watson, D. (ed.) (1985) *A Code of Ethics for Social Work: The Second Step*, London, Routledge and Kegan Paul.

Wolfensberger, W. (1972) *The New Genocide of Handicapped and Afflicted People*, New York, Syracuse University Training Institute (Available in Britain from CMH publications, 5 Kentings, Comberton, Cambridge, CB3 7DT).

## The numeric system

Some academic texts – both books and articles – will give details of sources in the form of 'footnotes' or 'endnotes'. In this form of citation, details of sources may be interspersed with notes about the text.[18] Such notes are usually used to present material that would interrupt the flow of the argument if it appeared in the main text. As a student it is probably best to avoid their use except in a thesis or dissertation.

Using the numerical system, whenever an author wishes to cite a source, she inserts a symbol (usually a number) at the point in her text where she wishes to make the citation. Full references appear either as 'footnotes' or as 'endnotes'. One potentially confusing feature of the numerical system is the liberal use of Latin abbreviations which make people look very clever but can confuse the uninitiated (see our discussion of not knowing on page 22):

'ibid.' is used to indicate that the current reference is to the same place as the previous one

'op. cit.' is used to indicate that the current reference is to a work already referred to.

For example,

1 Dingle, J. (2001) *Realism in the Imaginary World*, Dunscore, Hofflich Press.
2 Dingle, ibid.
3 Tortellini, F. (1977) *Pasta and the Italian Baroque.* Glyn Ceiriog, Dolan and Harris.
4 Costello, P. and Norris, R. (1854) *The Art of Pomposity, Ill Manners and Deception*, Staines, Plas Coch Press.
5 Dingle, op. cit.

### One list or two?

Sometimes students offer two lists at the end of an assignment. The first (which will often be referred to as a 'reference list') is a

---

18 Notes are either 'footnotes' which, like this one, appear at the bottom of the page, or 'endnotes' when they appear in a numbered list either at the end of the chapter or at the end of the book.

list of work they have cited, while the second (which will often be referred to as a 'bibliography') is a list of all the work that they think might have influenced what they have written. Sometimes both types of references are combined in one list, which might be labelled by either name. One very odd reason for this tactic is that some students seem to entertain the delusion that giving references to stuff that isn't cited in the text of their essay will offer protection against the charge of plagiarism.

Our view is that there is no point giving references to books and articles that might have influenced you unless you cite them in the text of your assignment because, unless you cite them, there is no evidence that you have read them, far less that you understand and have thought about them. An uncharitable teacher might conclude that doing so has more to do with the attempt to persuade her that you have read something than it has to do with the fact that you actually have read (and understood) something; and some students undoubtedly entertain the misguided notion that including references to sources they have not cited will fool those who read and mark their work into thinking that they have read and know more than they really have read and really do know.

## Make sure your references are accurate

You should take care that all information in references is accurate, particularly when the source is a published one, when you should always take the information for your reference directly from the source. To do otherwise indicates slovenly study habits. During the time that we were working on this book, one of us was irritated by a number of students who gave references that seemed to be to a book he had published. A couple got the book's details correct but managed to attribute it to an author with a name that resembles ours in some way, while another got both his name and the name of the book right, but the date of publication wrong. One, who got his name right, got the name of the book wrong. The point is that our name is not Fairbairne, Fairbun, Fairbarn, Fairbourne, Freebrain or Fairburn, but Fairbairn, and the book in question (which incidentally he wrote with Winch and not Wincher or Winche) is called *Reading, Writing and*

*Reasoning* (Open University Press 1996) and not, for example, *Reading, Writing and Thinking* (Oxford University Press 1998).

### Keeping an up-to-date bibliographical record

In order to allow you to give full and accurate references you will have to cultivate the discipline of keeping clearly labelled notes about sources. This will facilitate you in returning to material you have already consulted and in compiling a list of references cited. You should maintain notes about sources you have consulted in an alphabetically ordered list. You may choose to record this information in a computer database, or you may choose to use index cards, organized alphabetically by author in sections that relate to different aspects of your subject. Whatever method you use, you should record not only bibliographical information about each source – date of publication and other information that you will need in presenting your list of references – but also a few notes about the main ideas in each source. Care taken in cross referencing will allow you to relate different sources and track down your notes on different topics, even when some time has elapsed since you read them.

# PART 8: Where to read and when?

If you are to make good use of your time as a reader, it is important that as well as making careful decisions about what you should read and how you should read it you should try, where possible, to undertake your reading in the best conditions possible. In Part 8 we want you to think further about the best places and times – for you – in which to accomplish the reading you need to get through. Though we have nominally split what we want to say into separate discussions of *times* and *places* for reading, there is, in practice, a great deal of overlap between the two.

Throughout the book so far, we have made it clear that we do not believe there is a catch-all standard recipe for successful reading. In Part 3 we suggested that you should not accept anyone's advice as definitive in relation to reading. If the solutions you find and develop to the problems you encounter are to be as effective and helpful as possible, they must be your solutions. You may draw on ideas from a number of different places, including your teachers and fellow students, as well as from books like this one. However, part of their strength will be their uniqueness to you. This is perhaps most obvious when thinking about where and when to read, because it would be difficult to find two students with exactly the same preferences and peculiarities. For example, whereas one person may find it perfectly acceptable to read in the bath or even on the loo, another might be appalled at the idea. And while one person may find that, unless he has a perfectly clear table on which to lay out his books, a decent pen and an A4 pad on which to take notes, he cannot begin to read a word, another may not be able to open a book unless his lap top is switched on and ready to accept the notes he drums into it.

When it comes to making decisions about where and when to read it is important that you take control as far as possible. If people suggest that you read in particular places and at particular times, by all means try out their suggestions. However, if their suggestions do not work, do not persist with them, but look for your own best places and times. Try to notice which surroundings and times are helpful when you are reading. After all, the reading to be done is your reading and if you find a particular place really conducive to worthwhile encounters with books, then you should read there, whatever other people think. In Part 8 we want to encourage you to be creative in your choices about where and when to read, because when you are being creative and active in thinking about your reading, perhaps using some of the suggestions we make, you will be taking charge of your work. This we believe will help you to accomplish your reading tasks.

## WHERE TO READ?

We don't want to suggest any particular place as the best place to read. However, we want to share some of what we know and have experienced, about helpful and unhelpful places. As we have said, different places suit different people and you should experiment with a variety of locations, bearing in mind the need to ensure that you can read in the ways that you need to read, with as few unhelpful interruptions as possible. We refer deliberately to *unhelpful*, rather than *unwelcome*, interruptions, because some interruptions may be unhelpful, even though they are quite welcome. You know the kind of thing: 'I'm just popping out for a pint. D'you fancy coming?' or 'I've had enough of this; are you coming for a coffee?'

Conditions are rarely perfect for any kind of academic work, including reading. At times you may even find yourself entertaining the idea that there is some kind of conspiracy afoot, involving places and events as well as people, aimed at preventing you and your books from becoming friends. While you might find a particular place conducive to reading at some times, at others you might find it impossible to read there. Not only that, but the best place may be different depending on the kind of reading. For example, a café or pub might be a good place in which to flick quickly through a book to locate helpful information for an essay; however, it is less likely to be suitable for undertaking the detailed work that will be involved in actually gathering such information together.

You may find that reading in bed last thing at night is helpful for reading a short section of a book or article, or even a single passage that you think might give the answer to a particular problem. Sometimes reading a small amount about a difficult idea just before going to sleep can have a beneficial effect, almost as if, having read about it before you fell asleep, you then dream it into your understanding through the night. However, late night reading is likely to be less conducive to undertaking detailed and careful work. In a similar way, whereas (like one of us) you might find the bath a really good place for skip reading to assess the value of a book, you are unlikely to find it ideal for detailed reading, especially if you are inclined to fall asleep. One of us always does really focused reading of difficult passages while sitting at his computer. This allows him to dialogue easily with the material he is studying, using the computer to record notes both about what the author has said, and about his response.[19]

## Reading in familiar surroundings

Much of your reading will be undertaken in your own room, with your familiar furniture, belongings and distractions. This may make it a good place to read, because you feel comfortable there. On the other hand, it may make it just about the worst

---

19 In Part 6 we give an example of this kind of intensive reading in relation to a short passage from the work of Florence Nightingale.

place, because you know it so well that you are an expert on all the excuses for avoiding work – including reading – that it has to offer, and you can move seemingly effortlessly between distractions of various kinds. This is particularly likely to be the case if you are sharing a flat with a number of other students.[20]

## Reading in libraries

If there is one place that we tend to associate with reading, it is the library. And why wouldn't it be, since libraries are the source of most of the books we use? However, it would be unwise to assume that your university or college library will always be a good place in which to read. Though they can be friendly and helpful places for readers, libraries can also be a source of frustration and so you should expect to have to put in some work, in order to make the best use of your library as a reader (rather than as a borrower).

### Do you have a favourite place in the library?
As students we both found it useful to try to read consistently in the same places in the library, even trying to get exactly the same spots if possible.[21] Given our quirky minds you might not be surprised to discover that we often chose to work in areas devoted to subjects that were not the ones we were studying. For example, when one of us was studying geology as an undergraduate, he used to read in the philosophy section of the university library, yet when he was a postgraduate student in philosophy, he liked to read either in psychology or in law. Your choice of a favourite place in the library might be governed by a variety of factors, including the number of people who use different areas, and the attractiveness of the surroundings. You may, for example, prefer to work in an area that is fairly close to books that you are likely to want to consult, especially if it is relatively quiet. If it also has attractive views from the windows and is within striking

---

20 Perhaps you would like to make a list of all the ways in which you can distract one another, then try neither to be distracted by your flatmates nor to distract them.

21 We realize that this smacks a little of obsessionality, but in matters as important as study we think a healthy degree of obsessionality can be a good thing.

distance of decent coffee (to be used as a reward for getting particular bits of work done) then your mind may be made up.

When working in the library you may well find that different areas are helpful for different kinds of reading. For example, the kind of reading that we refer to as 'grazing', which we discuss in detail on pages 149–50, can only be carried out while standing next to the stacks on which you are grazing. On the other hand, you might find that you want to set up a reading post near the journal collection, if you are going to be spending a lot of time going to and fro with giant bundles of enormous journals. That way you can check out whether a particular volume is worth reading in detail, before lugging it back to your place.

Developing relationships with particular locations can turn them into your own personal workstations. Just as you habitually go to particular rooms or lecture theatres, or perhaps laboratories, for different classes, so your feet may easily take you to the workstation that is appropriate to your reading in each subject. If possible you should take particular notice of places in which you read successfully and try to return there soon. Success has a tendency to repeat itself.

*Libraries aren't always the best places to read*
There is so much coming and going, and there are so many possibilities for distraction, including, as we have already said, a source of decent coffee nearby (most good things in life also have a negative side), that for some people libraries may be the worst place to read. Indeed, for most people they will be the worst place in which to do certain kinds of reading, including the kind of detailed reading in which you are trying to mine deeply for information, struggling with unfamiliar concepts and ideas.

Some kinds of reading, however, are best carried out in libraries, including the kind of fast skimming that you might undertake in order to make a reasoned decision about whether a book or article is worth reading in detail. This is best carried out on the spot when you first find the source in question. Otherwise you are in danger of taking out books and journals (which tend to be bound together in volumes that most people can barely lift) simply because you think that they might contain something important. This can be a source of enormous disappointment if, after all your effort in lugging them home, you discover that they are useless for your purposes. Returning home from the library with a large pile of important looking books and journals can give you the warm and comforting feeling that you have done some decent work. However, unless you have already established that they contain material that will be useful to you, you may well be wasting time and energy that could have been better spent in reading one short article really thoroughly, especially if you have already taken the time to decide that it really will be useful.

*Grazing on library shelves*

There is one species of academic reading that can only really be carried out in libraries – the kind that we refer to as 'grazing'. This style of reading involves locating a library stack in which you are likely to find books relating to a topic in which you have some interest (perhaps by using the library catalogue) and then browsing among the books nibbling away at what you find, making decisions about books and journals you should spend more time looking at in detail, perhaps taking a few notes about interesting ideas. We cannot stress enough how useful this can be. Unorganized and strange though it may seem – it is indeed a pretty 'hit and miss' affair – grazing can produce enormous benefits in terms of books and journal articles that otherwise you might never have come across.

Grazing seems to us to be the print-based equivalent of 'surfing the net', though in our view (and we are not altogether technophobic) it is likely, for many years to come, to be somewhat more useful. For one thing, though there is no absolute arbiter of quality in printed sources – what is printed is down to the judgement of editors and reviewers or referees – there is at least some quality control in relation to most of what ends up in printed books and journals. The same is not true of much of the material that finds its way onto the Internet. Anyone can post material on the net and, except where you have good reason to believe in the veracity of what you read (as in the case of Internet journals which have similar reviewing procedures to paper journals), it would be wise to be somewhat circumspect in your use of such sources.

Another reason that we believe grazing on paper is perhaps more useful than surfing the net is that doing so is less time consuming. It is easier to dot between books that are displayed in front of your eyes than it is to browse on the much larger number of sources that are likely to be available on the Internet. It is also possible to skim and scan through printed text in quite different (and in our view faster) ways than it is to browse through electronic pages. This leads to a warning. Beware the temptation, arising from the fact that paper sources are easier to consult and read than electronic ones, to print out loads of stuff from your journeys through the Internet, in the hope and expectation that you will read them later. The undoubted pleasure of printing out a load of stuff from an Internet journal or other electronic source mirrors the warm and comforting feeling that we have suggested comes from returning home with a pile of important looking journals, giving the false impression that you have done some worthwhile work. In our experience, much of what people print off from the net turns out not to be worth the cost of the paper it was printed on. Better to take the time to ensure that the source in question really will be useful, before making a paper record of it.

We suggest strongly that you try to develop the habit of doing a bit of grazing (say 10–15 minutes) each time that you visit the library. Doing so will undoubtedly help you to find worthwhile material. You may find it particularly valuable to graze among the journals that are most central to your concerns.

## Reading in unfamiliar and strange surroundings

At times you might feel completely stuck with a piece of reading in a familiar situation, but find that a change of place or time makes it possible to overcome these difficulties. In this section we discuss a variety of examples of less familiar and unfamiliar places in which to read.

### *Reading in a cupboard*

Sometimes the best place to read is not the most obvious one, and sometimes the oddest places can provide a haven for reading that is both unexpected and welcome. For example, both of us at times sit and read on the stairs in our house, not because there aren't more obvious places, but because sometimes that is the best place to get out of the way and avoid being bothered by one another and by other family members. Even more odd, probably, is the fact that as an undergraduate, one of us once spent a considerable amount of time reading in a cupboard.

In Edinburgh, where he was studying, many of the big old flats have large cupboards called 'presses', not as big as a box room, but big enough to have a light inside, and with large shelves. He'd been having tea with a friend and moaning about the fact that he couldn't seem to find anywhere quiet and free from distraction in which to study when he stood up and said, 'I suppose I could always read in your press.'

Now this was admittedly a stupid thing to say and an even more stupid thing to do, but say it he did and what's more he did it (admittedly just for a laugh, such was his odd sense of humour). Picking up his books he walked through the hall, opened the press door and, jumping up, sat on a shelf at shoulder height and began reading. Several hours later when his friend brought him some food he realized that his stupid joke had produced a solution to the problem; by then he had done the first decent bit of reading he'd done for ages. And so he returned to the cupboard repeatedly over the next few weeks. This story is about a particularly odd choice of place for reading. We share it, not because we want to suggest that you should read in a cupboard, but in order to illustrate our view that in reading, as in all aspects of academic life, what is important is that you should find the best solutions for you, no matter how odd they might seem.

### Strange libraries

You should not limit your use of libraries to the university library, or to your departmental library, since you may find other libraries useful as places in which to read. Most cities have large central libraries and many are not only situated in very fine buildings that for some people might make them attractive places in which to read, but also contain decent collections of books. Even local libraries often have quiet areas in which you may find it possible to carry out serious reading. In addition most public libraries have some access to the Internet (though this probably has to be booked ahead of time and, depending on the location, there may be a charge).

Your choice need not be limited to public libraries, because it is most often possible to have some access to libraries in other universities and colleges, either through reciprocal arrangements with your own institution, or by payment of a fee. You may well find visiting a different library a liberating experience, though you should check before going that it has at least some of the material and facilities in which you are interested. Your own university library will be able to assist you in finding out both whether you can get access to the library of your choice and, if so, what you will have to do in order to arrange this (alternatively, you may find this information on the Internet).

When one of us was having a particularly bad time with a subject that she found especially boring and difficult – physiological psychology – she had the idea of carrying out some important reading in a library that she had always wanted to visit. During the long summer vacation she arranged to work in the University of Cambridge library while she was on holiday in Cambridge. The reading she wanted to carry out in relation to physiological psychology seemed somehow to be easier while she was there, perhaps because it was distant from the place where she had been experiencing the stress of work and study.

## Reading on journeys

How good are you at reading during journeys? For example, are you the kind of person who can take one book with them on a three-hour train journey and get engrossed for most of the journey? Or are you the kind of person who will have to take several pieces of reading with them? One of us, who travels several hundred miles by rail most weeks, is incapable of sticking to one subject during his frequent train journeys. Nevertheless he manages to get through significant amounts of reading on trains each week, because he decides ahead of time what he wants to get through and organizes that he will do a number of different reading tasks. These usually include some copy-editing of his own work, some correspondence or other reading he has to do for work, and a small piece of fairly detailed academic reading, as well as reading a newspaper and perhaps a chapter of a novel. Whatever kind of travelling reader you are, it is certainly worth putting in a little effort to plan the reading you hope to accomplish. Remember that reading for a short time can be worthwhile and plan a short section for reading on a brief journey.

Do you ever walk along the road while reading? Some people do, including one of us and our daughter (perhaps there is a genetic predisposition because Faith did it automatically, never having seen her father do it).

### Reading at work

Many students undertake paid work during vacations if they possibly can, and also work part-time during term. To some extent, this cuts down the possibilities for studying. However, the workplace is often a good setting in which to undertake significant reading, even though you may feel a little strange producing a book rather than a newspaper or a magazine at break times, depending on whether any of your colleagues are also students.

When one of us was a first-year undergraduate, he spent the summer working in a wool mill where he and the workmates in his team, who were also students, used to work like mad during the morning so that in the afternoons, having completed their quota of work, they could lie about among the bales of raw wool, reading. You are unlikely to have this amount of freedom. However, even though most holiday or part-time jobs do not allow you to arrange your work so that you can have stretches of time with nothing to do, most will have some slack time where you can squeeze in a bit of reading, perhaps all the better for being slightly illicit. Indeed, while you are engaged in temporary or part-time work you could find that, if you give it a chance, reading something serious between busy times becomes important to you, reminding you that the work you are doing is only temporary and not a career for life. This might be especially true if the job you are doing is boring and repetitive. This was certainly the case for one of us who decided to read Bertrand Russell's *The Problems of Philosophy* whilst working in a Dorothy Perkins shop.

A page or two of reading when you can sneak it in might be more valuable than a whole hour of reading when you have lots of time to spare, but little motivation. Even if you are in a job where there is little slack time, you will find that reading for a small part of lunch or tea breaks can be extremely worthwhile. And if you try doing a little serious reading during meagre meal breaks in a part-time or holiday job, you may find that what you have learned is consolidated during the next period of work, so that you gain in understanding, even as you earn your wages. This is particularly likely where the paid work you are doing is mindless and repetitive. You might even find that a break from intellectual activity enhances your ability to reflect on what you read about, and your ability to apply it to particular questions in connection with assignments.

## WHEN TO READ?

Just as important as finding the right place to read is finding the right time of day for reading. Whereas some people find that they read best early in the morning, others find that they can only get up the energy to read late at night. You have to find your own best time or times. Though it is always worth trying out suggestions that others make, you should not persuade yourself, or allow yourself to be persuaded, that just because someone else has found that a particular time of day is best for them to read, it will – or should – be best for you. There is little point, for example, in trying to force yourself to read late at night, if you know that after a certain time you have difficulty keeping your eyes open. Nor is there any point in trying to get serious reading done first thing in the morning if you know that until you've been awake for a couple of hours you can barely focus on the back of the cornflakes packet, never mind on an academic text.

Like most people, you will probably find that not only certain places but certain times suit you best for reading, just as there are best times and places for writing and talking and sleeping. If you are to be as efficient as you can as a reader, you will have to make decisions, not only about the best places, but also about the best times of day for particular reading tasks. There would be no point in trying to offer you prescriptions about these things. Rather, you will have to work at becoming tuned in to how you feel when you are reading, recognizing occasions when your reading is worthwhile and when it is not, making decisions about whether you can make things better by changing either the place in which you are reading, or by reading at a different time.

Do you ever find, as you read, that you are falling asleep, or feeling agitated or desperately hungry – as if you need to eat something right now before you faint with weakness? Even if you find a book interesting, you may find yourself distracted while reading it, simply because you are tired, fed up, hungry or psyched up about something else. This may happen because, even if you are motivated to read it, just at that moment it doesn't excite or interest you. In such a situation it would probably be wise to put the book away for a while. There is little point in expending energy in trying to read something that you don't have to read when you are finding it difficult to do so, and there is always a danger that, by persisting, you might put yourself off the idea of reading this text at all.

However, you should be aware of the possibility that you might find a pattern emerging in your behaviour and mood, which suggests that certain texts have the remarkable power to make you feel tired, depressed or hungry, thus making them impossible to read. You might even find yourself scrabbling about for excuses to avoid particular pieces of reading. If this happens too often, it would probably be as well to rethink the way in which you are approaching the texts in question, perhaps drawing up a plan of action for reading them, making sure that you are clear about what you want to gain from doing so. You might also want to consider whether the places in which you are trying to read these texts are the most conducive for the kind of reading you have to do in relation to them. For example, if they are full of detailed and complex argument, it is probably not a good idea to try to read them when there is a lot going on around you – for example in a crowded library, or in the lounge of your flat when there are other people around.

## Finding the best times and places for different reading tasks

Like us, you may find that some reading tasks are best accomplished at specific times of day. If so, it is worth trying to ensure, where possible, that you undertake reading of different kinds at the best times (for you). Doing so can limit the anxiety that you might experience when faced by a task that you anticipate being difficult, and might help you to get round to actually facing up to it. This can be enormously helpful especially when, as often happens, you discover that the beast in the cupboard (or between the covers of the book) wasn't so scary after all.

Not only do people differ in terms of the places they find most conducive to reading and find that different kinds of reading will be easier in different places, but most people will find that the best place in which to read will vary, at different times. So, for example, when one of us was studying psychology, there were times when she found it difficult even to enter the university library, almost as if she was suffering from library phobia. She managed to get over this problem by working out the best time of day to go to the library to work. This turned out to be around the time that most other library users were going off for tea, when she found she was able to get some really useful work done. It was not simply that the library was less crowded then, but also that the stress of working and getting through the reading that she had decided was necessary for essays and exams seemed to be reduced by working when others were taking a break.

## Have you tried doing it standing up? (or 'Reading when everyone else has gone to sleep')

In general, you will wish to be fairly comfortable when you are reading, but sometimes discomfort facilitates getting the work finished. Although it is not usually a good idea to read when you are too tired, we are aware that, in real life, as a student, this will be necessary at times. One of us was once reading a novel and was too tired to finish it, finding herself falling asleep as she approached the end late at night (at about 2.00 am). Determined to get to the end she made the unusual decision to read it standing up and successfully got to the end (admittedly leaning against the doorpost). From our limited research on reading academic texts standing up, it seems that it is significantly more difficult to fall asleep when upright.

## Reading while waiting for others

Mature students or others who have children might find that they can get some useful reading done while their children are involved in activities such as clubs or lessons of various kinds. For example, as a postgraduate, one of us often managed to make good use of the time that he spent waiting while one of our children was having swimming lessons by copy-editing his own work. Even if you are one of the majority of students who does not have children, you may find that there are other times in your week when you spend small pockets of time in unusual places, that you can use in this and similar ways. For example, you may find that you have such time while you are waiting for your partner at the squash club, or after a football or rugby match that you really didn't want to watch anyway. Actually you might even be able, surreptitiously, to use the time during the match to do so.

As in a number of other situations that we have discussed both in Part 10 and elsewhere, you might be able to make positive use of the fact that the time you have available while waiting for someone is limited. One way of doing this might be to decide that since you have very little time, you should focus on a very limited piece of reading – a couple of pages, or even paragraphs if they are particularly difficult. It can be liberating to know that you have only a very limited time in which to get something done, which can encourage you to set realistic and helpful goals.

## Reading on holiday

Do you read outside term time? Or do you think that you work so hard during term that you deserve a break during vacations? Whatever your answers to these questions, we think you should seriously consider doing at least a little bit of academic reading during your summer vacation, and we have no doubt at all that it is essential that you should do some during other, shorter breaks. After all, if we guess correctly (and we guess we do), like most students, you have more reading to do than it is humanly possible to get through in the time you have available. It thus stands to reason that if you want to do well, you will have to find space for reading wherever it can be found. Vacations can be ideal times to find such space, however busily you fill them with working to eke out your student loan, or enjoying yourself on holiday.

Carrying a book around on holiday can be a good idea, because it allows you to snatch reading time where you can. A short session of reading in one place in the morning, say the beach, and one or two sessions later in the day, perhaps in a café or beside the pool, can add up to a substantial amount of work pleasantly achieved. However, it is important to bear in mind that simply carrying a book around (however impressive looking the book) does not automatically transfer its contents into your memory, or the ideas it contains into your essay, by osmosis, or some magical process. The book still has to be opened, read and digested.

One reason that holidays can be good times for getting down to some concentrated reading, perhaps on a topic or text you find particularly difficult, is that during holidays you can often give yourself more varied and interesting rewards than you can manage in term time. A session of focused reading during which you address a particular question, or an issue that you have decided to focus on for the day, followed by a whole day of rock climbing, swimming, shopping, sunbathing (or what you will) with the satisfaction of having done some work, can seem an attractive plan. In a way this is similar to the way in which one of us organized his time during a week that he spent in a cottage in Scotland copy-editing a draft of this book. In exchange for the work he carried out between nine in the morning and three in the afternoon, the late afternoons and early evenings were given over to a series of enjoyable walks which, incidentally, set him up nicely for working late into the night.

Of course, reading on holiday has its problems especially during the long summer break. Two scenarios come readily to mind, each of which we know well, and each of which emphasizes how important it is to plan holiday reading if it is to be worthwhile. Neither makes a great deal of sense. One is the situation in which you end up abandoning all academic reading for the whole summer. The problem is obvious – you don't do any reading over the summer and therefore you are even further behind when you return to university at the start of the new academic year. The other possibility is that you find yourself lugging round a suitcase or box full of books all summer aiming to read them all, but become increasingly depressed as it becomes obvious that this is impossible, so that, in the end, you read virtually nothing. One problem here is that the summer is an ideal time to wallow in self-deceit by embracing the illusion that you need a clear day (when you don't have anywhere you simply must go, or anything you simply must do) before you can get some worth-while reading done.

# PART 9: Share your reading with friends

So far in this book we have been talking as if reading is always a solo activity. In Part 9 we want to suggest that sometimes making it into a group activity – something that you share with friends – can make it even more productive.

## SHARING READING

Sharing your reading with friends can give you opportunities to extend, develop and practise your skills as a reader. But how can you do this?

---

**How might you share reading with a friend?**     *Task 9.1*

Make a list of ways in which you could share your reading with friends and how it might be helpful to do so. Then compare your ideas to those we outline below, some of which you may find rather surprising.

---

Please don't allow yourself to dismiss these ideas out of hand, because they might seem difficult to organize, or because some of them sound so naff that you would find it embarrassing to suggest them to friends. They are all variations of approaches that we have used successfully with students, and that is why we would urge you to try using them.

## Share books and other texts

Most simply, given the cost of books and the difficulties that you are likely to find in borrowing them, you might join up with a group of friends to share out the costs of building a small collection, from which you can all 'borrow'. Alternatively, you could each buy one or two books from a reading list, and agree to pass them round – either on a rota basis or according to need. In either case, everyone will benefit from the availability of a wider range of sources. This would clearly be cost efficient, but it could also save you time that you might otherwise waste in looking for books that turn out to be unavailable. It could, of course, be extended to books and articles (that you might want to photocopy) that are referred to in lectures, and to those that you come across in the course of your work.

You might think that the kind of arrangements we suggest would be impossible to organize, but there is no reason why this should be so, though you will have to think carefully about which resources to share, where and how they should be stored, and how to arrange that you each have an equal opportunity to access them. Such problems are clearly surmountable, especially if the members of the group live in the same flat, or in the same block in the halls of residence. Other problems that might arise – for example when everyone wants to use the same book or article for a particular essay and the deadline is looming – will be no more pronounced than they would be in the case of a library book that was both in demand and in short supply. And using this strategy, you will at least have more chance of getting access to the material you need.

## Share out the legwork of reading

You and your friends might each agree to undertake a certain amount of reading for a particular essay and pool what you have found out; or you might agree to such a strategy in relation to a topic that has been covered in lectures. Alternatively, you might each agree to read one article, or a chapter from a set or recommended book, and to take and share notes about opinions expressed, evidence presented and arguments offered. Finally, you might share out responsibility for locating and reading sources referred to in class or on a reading list, or for researching into and reading about some aspect of an assignment. Obviously agreements of these kinds will be most successful if everyone is committed to doing their best, and problems could arise if one person always seems to do less work than everyone else.

If you are faced with a lengthy required or recommended reading list[22] and you have reason to believe that it (or some part of it) is worth investigating as fully as possible, it can be reassuring to share out the decision about which texts look most interesting or relevant. Agreeing with friends that you will each read different things, taking notes to share with one another, will allow you to cut down the amount of time you have to spend in mining for information. Of course, blindly accepting what your friends say about a text without checking it for yourself would involve a leap of faith and we would advise against this, however much you trust them, especially if you intend to cite arguments or examples from that text in an essay.

In any case, sharing reading in this way should never be about each person in turn taking on the role of a pack horse – carrying information to the others, who then store it away to use as a source of raw and unworked material with which to fill their essays and assignments. Rather, each member of your group should view himself as an explorer visiting an unfamiliar place – making detailed notes of the intellectual landscape, which he then shares with his co-explorers. It is as if each person draws a sketch map and offers a verbal guide to the main landmarks and significant features of the landscape of the text they have explored, thus facilitating the others in carrying out their own, more detailed exploration.

---

22 We say more about such lists on pages 87–90.

The information you gather during your journeys through agreed texts could be shared in a variety of ways. For example, accepting our suggestion from Part 1, you might meet over a bottle of wine, and take turns to guide your friends in a tour of localities where useful information is to be found in the texts you have read. Such tours might be virtual tours in the sense that the others don't actually go to the locations you discuss, or physical tours where, through guided reading, you actually introduce them to the text itself. Alternatively, you might make your notes available to one another, by emailing or circulating photocopies of them or, if you can arrange this, by copying word processing files directly to a shared space on the university's computer network.

The most obvious advantages of sharing out reading in the way we are suggesting are that everyone can gain some knowledge of a wider range of material than they would otherwise and, perhaps more importantly, that no one has to read all the material or even look it up. Reading as a team in which each member shares the hard graft of getting to grips with texts will mean that you can avoid reading some texts yourself, because you will discover without even opening them that they were not worth reading anyway. Imagine the bliss of knowing that you don't have to trek round the library looking for everything that appears on a reading list, or that has been referred to in class and you have decided is worth checking out. Think of the time you could save.

Of course, shared reading will not allow you to avoid reading texts that turn out to be worthwhile, because you will probably want to work with such sources yourself, and you will have to do this if you decide they are worth citing in your essays; we say more about this in Part 7. On the other hand, you will not have had to locate them yourself, and when you come to read them you will already have a good idea about what you want and expect to gain by doing so. As a result you will be able to commit more time to working on drafting and redrafting your assignments.

### Developing your ideas by sharing your reading with others

As well as helping you to cut down on the amount you have to read, sharing reading out among a group of friends can have a number of other positive benefits. For example, you may find that sharing what you have found out by reading is invaluable in developing ideas for your essays. Many university teachers believe that the best way to learn about something is to have to teach it, and in sharing what you have learned from your reading this is what you will be doing.

To use a metaphor that we introduced in Part 5, in a sense what you and your friends will be doing by sharing the results of your reading is filleting texts you have read, exposing the backbone, laying aside anything nasty that you find inside, and making obvious which parts are meaty and worth digesting, and which are likely to cause problems. This is a big responsibility and one that may scare you – what if you get it wrong? After all, it is possible to choke to death on the small bones from some fish and, depending on how they are prepared, some fish may be difficult to digest. Something similar is true of academic texts, which often contain ideas and facts that may be uncomfortable to handle as you try to swallow and then digest them. In such a case, you will have to be willing to admit to your friends that the text you have been working on has caused you difficulties and ask for their help in getting to grips with it. Despite such possible problems, there are many real benefits to be gained from sharing out reading in a group in which each member takes responsibility for bringing the others 'up to speed' on a text. These include:

i You will undoubtedly benefit from the work you have to do in preparing to report back to your friends, whether you do so verbally, or by making your notes available to them.[23] For example, you will benefit from organizing your account of what the author says and your own views of what she says. You will also benefit from the process of actually sharing this information.

ii Provided that everyone 'pulls their weight', it is likely that you will have positive and worthwhile conversations

---

23 We should perhaps make clear that what we are talking about sharing here is notes about texts, that are designed to help others to understand and read them, rather than notes for an essay. It would, of course, be unwise to share notes for an essay, which could lead to unwitting plagiarism, however careful you were to avoid simply copying what a friend intended to say.

about the things you have each read, which will help
you to absorb and understand both the ideas you have
read about and those you hear about.

iii Finally, having done the reading, thought about what
you have read, and found a way of sharing it with your
friends, you will be in a better position to use it in your
assignments.

### Share your views of something you all read: work as a reading group

Sometimes you and your friends might decide that a particular
text – say a chapter of a set book, or an article referred to in
lectures – is so important that you should each read it and then
meet to share and discuss your views. In some ways this would
be like being a member of a reading group of the kind we described on page 30, in which members read the same books then
meet to discuss their responses. Where the material you each
read is of an academic kind, some advantages will be similar,
including the camaraderie that comes from being part of a group
that has had the same or very similar experiences.

How you proceed will depend on a number of factors, including your other commitments and the length of the text (it is
important to realize that you could do this with anything from a
lengthy book down to a particularly difficult section or even a
single paragraph). Either you could agree to read the text independently and then meet up to discuss it, or you could meet
together, read it on the spot, and have your discussion immediately afterwards. In either case, provided that you acted in
accordance with copyright law, you could arrange to have individual copies of a section of text on which you chose to focus.

Working in a group in which each member reads the same text
*before meeting to discuss* it together means that you do not have
to take sole responsibility for understanding what is being said
(an advantage that is not to be sniffed at). But there are other
significant advantages including, for example, the fact that it gives
you the opportunity to share a number of different viewpoints –
a number of different 'takes' on the same information. Discussing
a difficult piece of text in a group, rather than merely allowing
it to swish around in a jumbled mish mash inside your head,

gives you the opportunity to clear up misunderstandings and uncertainties, and to develop a better understanding of what the author is arguing or reporting.

You might sometimes decide to read with one or more friends, taking turns to read aloud, with everyone looking at a copy of the text, if possible. The idea that you should consider reading out loud with friends might be surprising. Perhaps you think it sounds rather childish? Not so. There are very good reasons why reading aloud with friends can be worthwhile. This is why one of us often gets students to read to one another in pairs or in small groups in class, when they are working on examples and exercises. Doing so confers a number of benefits.

For example, it ensures that everyone in a group gets to the end of the text at the same time. It also gives people an opportunity to talk in front of their peers without actually having to commit themselves to a view or opinion, because the words they are reading belong to someone else. This helps some students (those who would usually sit back and allow others to do the talking) to get ready to discuss a piece of text. Having heard their own voice, even though they are just reading someone else's words, will often help such a student to develop the courage actually to say what he thinks. Finally, if you adopt this approach to shared reading of texts, it is likely that the views people share will be fresh and unaffected – in others words, they will be less likely to share elaborated views designed to impress one another, and more likely to share their immediate and authentic responses.

If you decide to read in a group, the way you approach your text will depend on its nature and your reasons for reading it. Sometimes you may read all the way through a passage or chapter before entering into a discussion. On other occasions you may decide to go more slowly, reading sentence by sentence, or paragraph by paragraph. Reading at the level of the sentence will often be appropriate if you are considering a literary work, or a work that contains complex arguments that are difficult to follow. On the other hand, reading a whole chapter might be necessary in the case of a social science book in which each chapter describes a distinctive approach to social research, or in the case of an academic music text in which each chapter discusses the distinctive characteristics of the music of a particular period.

When you undertake shared reading in relation to argumentative texts, in which the author is attempting to persuade you to believe in a theory or way of thinking about some part of the world, things will be different. In this case, in sharing your response to a particular piece of text with a friend or friends who have read it with you, you will be developing your general ability to view academic texts critically, seeing them for what they are – the results of some other human individual's work and imagining about their topic. As we argue repeatedly throughout this book, academic reading is never simply about absorbing what authors have written. Rather, in most instances, the process of reading argumentative or persuasive texts should be about developing your own ideas by pushing against and interrogating views expressed by the authors you read. The discipline involved in sharing reading with a friend is very helpful for developing this approach to texts.

In the case of densely argued texts, you may want to read the relevant passage together and then split up so that you can each attempt separately to identify and restate the main stages in the argument or arguments presented. Doing this can be helpful in getting to grips with difficult texts, whether they are difficult because of the complexity of the arguments, or because of the stylistic ineptitude of the author; it can also be helpful as a way of improving your ability to track and understand arguments. Not only that, but if you each work separately on a restatement of the main argument, then pool results, you have a much greater chance that you will arrive at a decent understanding. As the proverb goes, 'two heads are better than one', and if you are working in a bigger group, hopefully things will be better still.

## Developing reading skills with friends from a different subject

Finally, in what we have said so far, we have concentrated on sharing reading as a way of preparing academic work for your course. However, if your main aim is to develop your reading skills, you might want to consider doing so with friends who are studying in a different area. One possible benefit relates to the temptation to assume that because an academic is a significant figure in her field, what she says must be worthwhile. For some students the picture is even worse, because they are tempted to rely on the authority of almost anyone who has published about a topic, no matter where they have published it and whether what they have said has any merit. The advantage of reading material from your course with friends for whom your area of study is new is that they are likely to be less impressed by an author's reputation and may thus be more likely to spot or draw attention to incoherence, absence of clarity and weaknesses in arguments and evidence.

There are also, perhaps surprisingly, considerable benefits to be gained from shared reading of texts that have nothing to do with your own subject. In our experience, this is quite likely to happen naturally if you are sharing a flat with people who are studying other subjects. In the same way that you and your friends might borrow clothes or CDs, you might find yourself borrowing books, especially if your friends are excited about reading them. This is how one of us first came across the Spanish poet and dramatist Lorca, when she was living with a mixed bunch of students in Edinburgh. In other words, you might suddenly find that the books your flatmates or friends have to read somehow seem terribly attractive, even if previously you had no interest whatever in Spanish literature, astrophysics or ancient Egyptian toilet systems, or in the digestive tract or sexual habits of the land snail, for example.

The point here is that, like grass, the book or article on the other side of the fence is always greener (or seems more interesting). More seriously, reflecting on a subject that you are not studying as part of your course can be like going on a holiday. It can be good to get away from your everyday situation – to visit other places and other ways of life – and the same is true of academic life, where it can be good to get away from the familiar surroundings of your subject. This allows you to explore new territory and new ideas, and to sample new ways of thinking. In addition, expanding the range of things that you know about can only be a good thing, and you will probably be surprised at the extent to which there are overlaps in approach, in relevant factual knowledge and in ways of thinking, between subjects you used to assume had absolutely nothing in common.

## A range of benefits

We predict that you will find shared reading beneficial in a number of ways and we have tried to draw your attention to a few of these. No matter whether you adopt one of these approaches or some other approach that we have not discussed, and no matter whether you and your friends read the same or different things, you will be able to share your responses to texts. It is a bit like having a workforce to help you to build the framework or scaffold of understanding, on which you hang the ideas you are deriving from your shared reading. Any kind of shared reading is partly about having the opportunity to learn from other people's strategies, from their approaches to scaffolding, and from their ways of organizing what they have learned. These are general benefits that can arise, whatever kind of shared reading you undertake and whatever kinds of text you choose to read, and they are worth striving for. One of us is still partly convinced that the reason her good friend Ann ended up with a first, while she only achieved an upper second, was that Ann was incredibly efficient at condensing her notes as the final exams approached. Perhaps if they had engaged in shared reading, she would have been able to pick Ann's brains and further develop her own skills in this essential area.

| Read with a friend/with a group of friends | Task 9.2 |
| --- | --- |

Now that you've read a little about what we think you might be able to gain from shared reading, try it out. Find a reading task that you have been putting off, or having difficulty with – say an article or chapter, or even just a single passage. Then persuade a friend, or even better a small group of friends, to share the reading with you in one of the ways that we have suggested. You might, for example:

- share out the reading between you
- agree that you will read the text independently and discuss your responses
- read and discuss the text together.

No doubt some and perhaps many readers will reject the ideas we have suggested as impractical. Some may protest that they have no real friends in their course and that therefore it isn't possible for them to get involved in shared reading activities of the kind we have described. On the other hand, someone in this situation who is brave enough to suggest such reading activities to others might well find that doing so is a good way of 'breaking the ice' and fostering friendships. Indeed, instigating a shared reading group might well help to lay the foundations for relationships that continue well beyond university. In any case, unless you have no friends at all (and this seems unlikely), you may still be able to benefit because, as we have suggested, you might form a group with people who are not on your course. And even if you really have no friends you might like to prepare a report on a piece of reading for an imaginary audience, or perhaps for the person in your class you would most like to be your friend. You could even try giving it to them and asking whether they would be willing to comment on it; if you do, you might find that they feel flattered that you have asked for their advice.

Others may argue that hard-working students maintain momentum through the spirit of competition that develops between them and their peers, and that this will inevitably mitigate against cooperation of the kind we are suggesting. In other words, we anticipate that some readers will believe that it is impossible to set up shared reading, because they can't imagine other people wanting to do it. They may well be right; some students may be so mean spirited that, in the words of the old adage, they are willing to 'cut off their nose to spite their face'. In our experience, however, most students are generous with their ideas, willing to share and willing to learn from one another. We hope you are one of them.

We have not tried to offer a programme of activities. Rather we have offered a series of suggestions about ways in which sharing with friends can make reading an easier, more cost- and energy-effective business. Your fellow students are one of the most valuable resources to which you have access. Not only can they fill you in on lectures and reading that you miss, they can also help you to understand things that you do not understand – and to feel good about understanding things that they do not.

Even if you do not proceed in exactly the ways we have suggested, we hope you will take on board our main suggestion – that sharing reading with your friends and discussing what you read with them can be immensely beneficial to all aspects of your development as a student.

# PART 10: Reading your own work

In Part 7 we suggested that among other things you can improve your writing by improving the ways in which you read what others have written. More surprisingly, perhaps, we believe strongly that you can improve your writing, by working at changing the ways in which you read your own work. In Part 10 we want to talk about this important though often neglected aspect of reading as a student.

## DRAFTING AND REDRAFTING YOUR ESSAYS

Attempting to improve the ways in which you read what others have written is self-evidently worthwhile. It is perhaps less obvious what there is to gain by working at improving the ways in which you read your own work.

---

**Why would you want to read your own work?**  *Task 10.1*

Make a list of the reasons that you might have for reading your own work – other than to give yourself the opportunity of enjoying your own beautiful, crisp, clear prose – of basking in the glory of being such an accomplished writer. In doing so think also about whether there are any differences between the way in which you read other people's work and the way in which you read your own. Is there even, perhaps, a difference between the ways in which you read your own work, for different purposes? Finally, list the problems, if any, that you have in reading your own work.

---

Learning to read your own work better is perhaps the most important thing you can do if you want to become a better writer, because the work you will have to do in drafting and redrafting essays and other assignments is arguably the most important part of writing. Anyone can write down a string of words and with luck they will join up into sentences and paragraphs that say something worthwhile. The real skill, however, is in deciding how to make them communicate as well, as simply, as clearly and as elegantly as possible.

When you are writing essays and assignments of other kinds, it is a good idea to draft and redraft your work as often as you can. Working on successive drafts will enable you to develop your point of view, adding and juggling ideas, rethinking arguments and examples. Doing so will allow you gradually to develop your ideas in response to the question or task you have been set, and to make decisions about how best to present them. It will also help you to decide what further reading and research you can most usefully undertake in order to improve your text.

This is a more helpful and less harrowing way to work than doing what you take to be all of the necessary reading and research before rushing the writing of your essay in the last days (or perhaps even the last hours) before the submission deadline, as you try desperately both to work out what you want to say and to find a way of saying it. Leaving writing tasks until the last minute is surprisingly common among students. It is to be avoided because it does not leave time for drafting and redrafting and may thus lead to work that is full of errors in language and style. Even more significantly, perhaps, it also involves a level of pressure that most people cannot bear. Even if you are the kind of person who works best under pressure (and many people do, including both of us), it is unwise to place this amount of pressure on yourself, because doing so is likely to result in poorer work than you would otherwise have been able to produce. Very few people (if any) are capable of writing well without going through the process of writing, reading and revising a number of drafts.

### Read your work as if it was written by someone else

When, as part of the process of drafting and redrafting, you are reading your own work, it is easy to allow your familiarity with your text to fool you into thinking that it is well written – relevant, logically set out, non-ambiguous, clear and coherent, even when it is not. One way of getting past this familiarity is to make sure that, wherever possible, you begin work on written assignments far enough in advance of the submission date to allow you to leave them aside for a while between drafts; doing so can help you to approach your work with the fresh eyes that are necessary in order to allow you to spot errors and places where your text can be improved. Another way of tackling the problems that familiarity with your own text can cause is to enter into the imaginative game of reading it as if it had been written by someone else.

Making the attempt to read your work as if you are unfamiliar with it can help you to read it more carefully. There is a tendency (and we all suffer from it), when you are familiar with a piece of text because you wrote it, to fail to read it properly, and to skip over words, sentences and even whole passages, because you know what they say (or think you do; what you really know is what you intended to say). All too often this will happen without your noticing what is going on – until, that is, you come to your senses several pages further on and realize that you can't remember getting there. This is a special case of a problem we referred to in Part 4, where we suggested that you should approach academic reading with specific questions in mind, because this can help you to avoid falling headlong into the text, allowing yourself to be carried along with the flow, oblivious to what is being said. The problem is particularly pronounced when we are reading our own work, when it is all too easy to fail to spot mistakes. For example, it is easy to skip past repeated words and and phrases; places where words missing; places where you have used the wrong wood; misuses of words; places where you have make a mistake with tense; typoss (that is, apparemt mistakes in spelling or in the use of words that are actuallt the reslut of mistake on typung) as well as genuine mispelings; mistakes in punctuation? and grammatical error.

Technical errors in spelling, punctuation and grammar are irritating. However, they are perhaps less important than a number of other kinds of mistakes. For example, unless you are able to read your work as if you have never seen it before, you may fail to spot occasions when your examples or illustrations are weak or inappropriate, however entertaining, enjoyable or interesting they may be. In addition you may fail to spot occasions where your style is clumsy or boring. One particular example of this would be occasions where you have overused particular words, or have used them, for example, in constructing particular examples in illustrating the particular points you wanted to make about particular examples, for example. Another would be where lack of attention to detail might lead you (as it leads most of us at times) to develop the habitual use of certain words and phrases, more as a kind of stylistic 'tic' or 'mannerism' than because they are either necessary or helpful in making your points. Very often such tics add nothing at all. Consider, for example, the use of words and phrases such as: 'Literally'; 'Ultimately'; '. . . the fact that'; 'And so . . .'; 'It would seem that . . .'; 'It has to be said . . .'; 'Of course'; 'In light of . . .'; 'At this moment in time'. The use of such phrases is often useless and serves no purpose.

---

**What stylistic tics do you have?**      *Task 10.2*

Get out some of your old essays and read them over quickly, for one purpose and one purpose alone – to spot tics and mannerisms. If you have none, you deserve a medal. However, it is unlikely.

We all have stylistic mannerisms, which somehow seem to mul-
tiply unless we are uncommonly vigilant in removing them from
our work as we draft and redraft. You might find it amusing to
look out, as you read this book, for mannerisms of which we are
as yet unaware. If you spot any, we invite you to bring them to
our attention by writing to us, care of the Open University Press
at the address inside the front cover of this book. Then in the
next edition (if the book reaches a second edition) we will undertake to excise them and also to acknowledge your help in improving our writing. When he was copy-editing an earlier draft
of this book for us, our son had great fun in putting circles round
every instance where we had used (or where one of us had used;
the other claims that she would never do it) the words 'And so'
or the words 'Of course'. No doubt some of these remain, but
hopefully they are now thin enough on the ground.

   More importantly, perhaps, unless you are able to read your
work as if it was not your own, you may miss places where the
evidence you cite in support of your point of view is not strong
enough to do the job you want it to do, and where arguments are
weak or incomplete. It is especially important that you should
ensure that your arguments do not have missing steps, because
it is too easy to fall into the trap of thinking that you have said
all that is necessary, when in reality you have omitted a step or
steps. Consider, for example, the following argument:

> Out of town shopping centres should all be pulled down,
> because apart from the fact that they are usually ugly places,
> they lead to the death of town centres and shopping in them
> contributes to global warming.

We don't know what you think about out of town shopping
centres or global warming, but we have some sympathy for this
writer's feelings. However, neither the fact that he feels strongly
about the issue nor our sharing his view proves how right he is,
just as the fact that you disagree with an argument or parts of
an argument presented by an author does not demonstrate that
it is weak.

   As a piece of persuasive writing, this brief argument about these
important social and environmental issues lacks a certain amount
of detail. In particular, no link is made between shopping in out
of town shopping centres and global warming. Presumably the

author is taking account of the many extra miles that most of those who shop out of town have to drive in order to do so, with consequent effects on the amount of exhaust fumes that are discharged into the atmosphere etc. The author of this brief argument has omitted some crucial steps in attempting to make his point, and the fact that we were able to guess at what he meant says more about us and our general knowledge than it does about his skill in either the construction and presentation of written arguments, or in copy-editing.

| **Reading critically** | *Task 10.3* |
| --- | --- |

Try reading the following extract from a conference paper that one of us presented a year or two ago. We have altered it by introducing some errors in spelling, punctuation, paragraphing and so on. Read the passage critically, as if you didn't write it (you didn't), and mark on it the ways in which you would change it to improve it. Then take a look at the version that was finally read at the conference, which appears on page 199, and see how many of the changes that you considered necessary, appear on the finalized text, and how many of the changes that do appear you did not decide were necessary.

You will probably find it a lot easier to get stuck into this piece of text than you find it to do the same to your own work. What you need to do in the future, whenever you read your own work, whether you are copy-editing or proof-reading, is to try to recall some of the glee that you experienced in spotting the mistakes in this passage, and try to recreate it in looking at your own text.

### Resolving the paradox; some suggestions
How ultimately, can we resolve this parradox – that effective nursing requires closeness and involvement of a kind that leads inevitably, to hurt which, in turn, leads to the risk, to the likelihood even, of less good and effective nursing? And what could you do in order to recognize and deal with or at least address, the hurt that nurses experience? And why should you do this? Why should you address the problems of hurt in nurses, when resources and

care are limited and there are others – the patients that you
are employed to look after and who trust you to look after
them well – who also need your care?
Well in the end, it would seem that one of the most
important reasons might be, that because you are caring
people, you care about nurses as colleagues, as members of
your profession, or maybe you should do it just because
they are human beings, another iportant reason might be
that you the recognize that in the end if nurses are less
efective because of the hurt that they experience in their
practise, they will be less able to care for the people in their
care.
Ultimately in my view since we can't get rid of the risks of
hurt without at the same time sacrificing important aspects
of nursing that are centrally important to its ethos, and to
its overall general effectiveness, we must attempt to address
the hurt that nurses experience, in other words addressing
the problems of hurt among nurses might in the end be
about caring for patients as much as it is about caring for
the nurses who care for them.

As a result of stress and hurt, nurses need to be supported
– they need support of the kind that might be engendered
in a co-operative team, working closely together. But
ultimately it would seem to be true that they need more
than this they need opportunities to share their hurt to tell
it and give it up. Mead (1995b) talks of the way in which
she has come to think of the moral and emotional burdens
that we suffer as being rather like elephants that we carry
around with us. She tells how during her work with
student nurses she likes to try her best to give them lots of
opportunities to share their hurt and upset and how being a
good supervisor she gathers up this upset and hurt (the
'elephants' her students have been carrying about with
them) and having allowed her students to off-load their
elephants she takes them home with her, strangely enough I
do just the same thing with my student teachers.
Unfortunately as is the case with everyone who is
accommodating in the matter of helping others to deal with
the elephants they have been carrying round on their head
Professor Mead has to find some way of off-loading the

elephants she has been carrying about with her all day that she has picked up from her students when she enters home in the evenings which is where Mr Mead comes in, how he deals with the elephants to which he is exposed, I have yet to discover, but my guess is that, being a good husband he begins visibly to bow down under the load as dinner proceeds, something similar is true of Mrs Fairbairn as I have noticed on the too frequent occasions when I have taken home a particularly heavy load of elephants that I have picked up from other people. Nurses, like everyone else in the caring professions, need to be able to unload the elephants that they are carrying, in a way that does not harm others.

And there is a multitude of people whom one might harm by off-loading the stress one has accumulated even in an averagely stressful day.

One's spouse, one's friends, one's colleagues, the man who carves us up at the traffic lights when we are hurrying home, one's clients and patients. One way of offering such care and support is clinical supervision, because one of the functions of such supervision must be to enable nurses to survive and grow not only as nurses but as people, because it is only by being personal in their work that they can realize their potential as carers. And so my view is that nurses who are hurting can be clinically efective but that their clinical efectivenes must be underpined by care for them as people.

Professionalism in nursing involves not only the application of clinical knowledge and skill combined with the ablity to make objective and rationale judgments, but the ability and willingness to relate as a person, as a real, whole person, to one's patients as whole people.

(Metamorphosed passage taken from Fairbairn, G. (1995) 'Can nurses who are hurting be clinically effective?' Paper presented at an international conference to celebrate the 150th anniversary of the birth of Florence Nightingale, University of Swansea)

### Be your own severest critic

Whenever you write as a student, take the time to read your own work carefully and painstakingly. In doing so you should adopt the persona of your own severest critic, who will, we hope and believe, turn out to be your best friend, as he spots the blunders you have made in successive drafts and helps you to tidy up your essay or assignment ready for submission. Perhaps you should try this out now, even if you are in the habit of reading your work frequently as you write.

---

**Being your own severest critic**                                **Task 10.4**

Before reading on, look out an old essay or assignment – or a draft of an essay or assignment on which you are currently working. Since you are going to write on it, you may want to make a photo-copy. Now pretend that someone else wrote it and read it critically. Really get stuck into it, bearing in mind questions such as these:

Could changes to layout and typography make it easier to read? (Font, print size, justification, spaces between para-graphs, organization of headings and subheadings etc.)

Does it have mistakes in grammar, spelling or punctuation?

Does the introduction work? (It does have an introduction doesn't it?)

Does it have a conclusion? Does the conclusion conclude anything?

Is it clear and coherent? Is it well argued?

Are any examples and illustrations interesting, helpful and necessary?

Is it obvious why other authors who are cited, are cited?

Are references given correctly, to the best of your knowledge?

Are quotations that are used necessary and/or helpful? Is it obvious why they are included?

Where could the author of this essay (you've forgotten for the moment that you are the author) improve it? How?

(See also the box on pages 184–5 about questions to bear in mind when copy-editing your text.)

---

How was it for you? We would be surprised if you found it easy. If you did, it probably means you were not being hard enough on yourself. The trouble is (and it is shared by most, if not all authors, even those who are very experienced) that once we have given birth to an idea, example or argument, to a beautifully crafted phrase or sentence, there is a great temptation to wallow in the glory of having done so. You will probably find that this temptation exists even when your ideas and arguments and ways of writing are not at all beautiful, or well constructed or even relevant (though as their creator you may be convinced that they are). This is especially likely when you feel you have 'sweated blood' and, as a result, have begun to think that what you have written has got to be good because you've worked so hard on it. Not only that but there is a cosiness about reading your own work, a feeling of belonging, that can lead you to fail to notice its ineptness (when it is inept), its weaknesses (when it is weak), or the fact that it is more longwinded or complicated than it needs to be, in order to do the job you are asking it to do.

Unless you are able to read your own work with, as it were, new eyes, taking on the guise of one for whom meeting your work is a totally new experience rather than a visit to an old friend, you are in danger, as all authors are, of sending it into the world equipped with arguments and ideas that are weak and/or inappropriate. In the case of professional authors, what is at stake when they write professionally is their credibility with their peers. That is why we are, frankly, surprised by the rather low quality of writing that is produced by a huge number of academics in most subjects. As a student, what is at stake is perhaps even more important, because if you fail to make your work as good as it can be, you are in danger of failing to impress your lecturers. And failing to impress them can result in lower marks than you might otherwise merit.

## Read your work aloud

One of us always reads work that is intended for public perform-ance, out loud – usually many times – before actually delivering it at, say, a conference or guest lecture. (Not only does he read it aloud, he also reads it aloud in front of a mirror – or a live audience if he can get one.)[24] This may sound like an indication of a serious mental health problem, but in truth there are very good reasons for it. Partly it is about rehearsing the theatrical event of conference presentation. For example, it allows him to practise his delivery – to decide when it is appropriate to look up at the audience, and when it would be appropriate to pause and allow the possibility of an aside from the main thread of his text.

We would suggest strongly that you should consider adopting the practice of reading your work aloud at times. It will be particularly helpful if you are a postgraduate who has opportunities to present work to colleagues, or an undergraduate who at times is required to read your work to others, in seminars or tutorials. Please don't allow yourself to feel that it is idiotic to read aloud when there is no one to listen other than yourself, a mirror or even your next door neighbour's rosebush (though in the latter case, you may wish to avoid your neighbour overhearing). If you try it, you will discover that the experience of reading your academic work aloud is quite different than that of reading silently.

In particular, you will find that sometimes reading your academic work out loud can help you to spot mistakes in a way that reading silently would not. For one thing there is no possibility of reading your work aloud while skipping through the text in the way that there is when you are reading silently. Hearing the sounds of the words that you have written as you speak them can be helpful in the attempt to work out whether they actually make sense. A variation would be to get someone else to read your work aloud to you. You might find that you have to offer them an inducement to do this, for example, by entering into a reciprocal arrangement with a friend. However, it will probably be well worthwhile. Having your text read aloud by someone else is similar to, but different from, reading it aloud yourself and it can be very useful. For example, it can help in identifying places where it does not make sense, or at any rate where the sense does not flow as easily as it might, because it gives you an opportunity to listen to your work almost like an outsider and to assess it as if you were hearing it for the first time.

---

24 Our cat, Jackson, has become terribly bored with hearing about health care ethics, while remaining still quite interested in educational work.

**Copy-editing and proof-reading**

In order to be able to work efficiently on your written work, you will have to learn to read it in two distinct, though clearly related, ways.

First, you will have to learn to read it in the way that a copy-editor in a publishing house will read the text of a book or article.

Secondly, you will have to learn to read it in the same way that a proof-reader in a publishing house will proof-read texts.

Each of these approaches to critically reading your own work may benefit from the practice of reading it slowly and word for word. Reading like this is a simple way of slowing down the process of proof-reading or copy-editing to a pace at which you are less likely to skip over passages, failing to note mistakes, because, as the author, you are so familiar with the text. A really useful way of ensuring that you read your own work carefully, both when you are developing your text and when you are checking it, is to use a marker – a piece of paper or perhaps a ruler – which you place below the line you are reading and move down line by line. Though it may have echoes of reading in early childhood, we find this an effective device. Try it.

*Copy-editing*

Copy-editing is focused at the level of content. It involves reading a text closely in order to check that it makes sense and does not contain omissions; ambiguities; inconsistencies; peculiarities of style; spelling or grammatical errors, or mistakes in the use of words. It can also involve spotting places where further development of an idea or the introduction of new ideas may improve the text.

The skills that are necessary for efficient copy-editing take time to learn, but they are skills that will improve your writing as you develop critical ability. They overlap with some of the skills that you should be developing and using whenever you read material written by others in the active and critical way that we described in Part 4. They also mirror the critical ways in which rigorous markers will read your work. One of the things that you will have to learn, as a student, is to read the comments written on your essays by the people who mark them, in a way that allows you to benefit from them, rather than being destroyed by them. We hope for your sake that you have, or will, come across such markers early in your academic life, because they will help you to realize both where you are going wrong and where you are getting things right.

There are, of course, great differences between markers in terms of the level of detail at which they work, the amount they write, and how helpful it is. However, the likelihood is that at least some of your lecturers will write incisively and helpfully, not only about the content of your essays including the extent to which you have addressed the question you were set, but about your writing style. It is important that you develop a good attitude towards those who are marking your work, one in which you are willing to learn from what they have to say, even when you disagree with some of it. It is too easy to develop poor attitudes towards those who mark your work, thinking that they are being unreasonable, when perhaps they have bent over backwards in the attempt to be as generous as they can.

Some markers will be unreasonably hard and some will be unfair. However, unless you come across consistently unfair practice on the part of a particular lecturer, it is probably best just to learn what you can about their idiosyncrasies and try as far as possible to address them next time around. In the end, if the person who is responsible for awarding you marks suggests that you should do certain things, it is worthwhile doing them, if only as a means to better grades; and it is likely that much of the time what they say will be well founded, no matter what you think of it.

---

**In copy-editing your text, you will have to read it as if you did not write it, with questions such as these in mind:**

Does it make sense? Is its main thrust clear?

Is it well structured and easy to follow? In other words, are points of view and arguments presented in the best order, and are there sufficient sign posts to allow me to find my way round?

Are points made clearly and succinctly? Is there sufficient information to allow me to understand what the author is saying?

Is any of what is said ambiguous?

Is any of what is said irrelevant? Are there any places where the text wanders from the main point into interesting but irrelevant side issues?

Is the text coherent? That is, does it 'hang together'? Is it inconsistent at times?

Does the author (in this case, you) fulfil the promises that she/he makes? For example, if she/he says that she/he will offer arguments, does she/he in fact offer them, or does she/he, rather, merely make an assertion – that is, state a point of view (however forcefully)?

Are the arguments used valid and strong enough to support the points of view offered?

If examples and illustrations are used, are they interesting and appropriate?

Is good use made of every single word, or do some words serve as 'padding', bulking up what would otherwise be rather a thin piece of work?

Are there stylistic 'tics' or 'mannerisms', that is, words or phrases that appear over and over again, whether or not they convey meaning? If they do convey meaning, could a more apt word or phrase be substituted?

Is there any unnecessary repetition in what is said?

(See also the box on page 180 about questions to bear in mind when being your own worst critic.)

We suggest that you use these questions in reading through each draft of your essays or assignments. In addition, you might care to stop at the bottom of each page and ask yourself the general question: 'How does this page and each paragraph on it help to answer the question that is being addressed?'

Finally, it is important to draw your attention to a problem that can arise for copy-editors who work on successive drafts of the same piece of writing. Boredom can lead a copy-editor to do a less good job than she would do otherwise, both because once she has read a piece of text several times it can be difficult to develop enthusiasm for doing so again, even if it has undergone substantial changes in the meantime, and because it can interfere with her ability to spot mistakes. When you are not only the reader but also the author, the problem of boredom is doubly important, because it is added to the problems that arise simply from familiarity with the text because you wrote it. This is the reason that we would strongly recommend that, where possible, you should stagger your work on assignments over as long a period of time as possible. In this way you can arrange that having completed a draft you can leave it aside for a few days, or perhaps even a week or two, before returning to it, when it will often be easier to read it again with 'fresh eyes'.

### Proof-reading

Proof-reading is closely related to copy-editing but has a different focus and takes place much later in the writing process; in publishing it involves checking 'proofs', that is, the pages that have been prepared for printing. Although, when you are proof-reading your work, you will occasionally spot simple grammatical errors, it will not usually be about making adjustments to style or content. Rather, proof-reading should involve reading your text with an eye on the more technical aspects of writing, that is punctuation, spelling and general presentation, including layout or typography.

When you are proof-reading your work you will find it helpful if you are able to read so far as possible as if the material you are reading is devoid of interest or meaning, because what you are primarily interested in is assessing whether technical details such as punctuation and spelling are correct. Indeed it is important, when you are proof-reading, that you should not allow meaning to come between you and the mistakes you are trying to spot.

Unlike copy-editing, proof-reading can become quite a quick process, although you should not aim for speed at the cost of accuracy. Indeed, although it involves reading texts very closely, in a way it does not involve looking for mistakes, but simply allowing them to reveal themselves to you. It is a little like picking blackberries or looking for beautiful pebbles on a beach, because after a while you don't actually have to look for them – rather they seem to jump up to meet you. Similarly after practice, technical errors in a piece of text will simply stand out because they don't look right.

Unfortunately some people will never spot spelling mistakes, no matter how madly those spelling mistakes jump up and down and tear their hair and shout and scream to be spotted. If you are one of these people, you must make sure not only that you make use of the spellchecker on your computer (assuming that you use a computer to write your work) but that you engage a friend as a human spellchecker because spellcheckers do not spot all mistakes.[25] Actually, it is worthwhile engaging such a person, even if you are quite good at the technical aspects of writing, because you are bound (well almost bound) to make at least some silly mistakes and to fail to spot them, however good you are.

### Copy-editing and proof-reading: two sides of the same coin?

We have written about copy-editing and proof-reading as if they are two separate processes, but in reality there will be a lot of overlap between them, and much of the time when you are reading your own work you will do both things at the same time. As you read and revise successive drafts of your work you will spot errors in spelling, punctuation and grammar even if you are reading primarily for content and sense; it is always best to note corrections whenever you see them, correcting them in your text as soon as possible, rather than leaving them till the last minute.

Don't allow yourself to fall into the trap (as some students do) of thinking that you can sort out all the problems and mistakes at the end, just before you submit your assignment or essay; proof-reading text is a time consuming affair and it usually takes

---

25 For example, although you might expect that it wood, a spellchecker would not spot all off the mistakes in thus foot note. When we invited our spellchecker to look at this page, it pointed out that 'foot note' should be spelled 'footnote'; to bad then that it did not spot that 'off' should have been spelled 'of'. Off course, strictly speaking, this is knot a spelling mistake but a grammatical won because rather than just bring misspelled, it is the wrung ward. Nor, of coarse, would most spellcheckers pickup the mistakes in the remainder of this footnote, including 'wood', 'to', 'won', 'knot', 'bring', 'wrung', and 'coarse', 'two' and 'ward', because these two are the wrong woods.

several readings to get things right, or as right as they can be. This is as foolish as thinking that you can do all your reading first and then do all the writing in one great splurge of activity. However, as a general rule, dedicated proof-reading of your text – in which all you are doing is looking for technical 'bloopers' – is best carried out in the later stages of writing and it is most important with the final draft.

---

**Don't tamper with style or content while proof-reading your final draft**

When proof-reading a final draft, avoid lapsing into copy-editing mode.

- Correct spelling, punctuation and obvious mistakes in grammar.
- Do not be tempted to make last minute changes to style and content.

To ignore this advice is to tread on dangerous ground.

Last minute changes are almost certain to introduce technical and/ or stylistic errors, which will tarnish your work and may render parts of it incomprehensible.

**Be warned!**

---

Having developed the ability to read your own work painstakingly in the ways we have described here, you may want to offer to undertake similar work in relation to your friends' essays and assignments and to invite them to do this for you. Doing so will be helpful for everyone concerned.

# Postscript

## GETTING ROUND TO READING

Our objective as authors has been to offer guidance concerning ways of thinking about reading and its relationship to other activities in which you will have to engage as a student, along with practical advice about ways to improve your reading performance. Much of this advice seems so obvious to us that at various points in writing the book we found ourselves wondering why it should be necessary to write it down. We had to keep reminding ourselves that the initial impetus for *Reading at University* was contact with students, and our experience of the difficulties that they have as readers. It is because we remember how difficult it *can be to get through all the reading* that you have to do (and all the reading that you don't have to do, but think you should do) that we have aimed to offer guidance about making the best use of the limited time available. If you change the ways in which you think about reading and the ways in which you read, you will become a better, more focused and efficient reader.

Other than the sheer volume of reading to be undertaken, perhaps the most difficult part of reading is simply getting round to it when there are so many more attractive options – talking to friends, going to the pub, cleaning the toilet or taking the dustbin out (when you don't feel like reading, almost anything is an attractive option). In reading, as in writing, getting started is often the hardest part, and you will probably find that this is especially true when time is limited or even more precious than usual. The problem is that such times are all too frequent. For example, who wants to get down to some serious reading when they've just taken an exam, or finished an essay, or sat through an incredibly boring lecture, or just got home from their part-time job in the Student's Union bar or . . .

It is because getting started is such a significant problem that we want to end by giving some advice about ways of coaxing yourself into reading when the reading task in hand is a daunt-ing one. In Part 4 we suggested that, at times like these, a good way of encouraging yourself to get going is to set your sights low, aiming only to accomplish very little (see 'You don't have to be great to get started, but you have to get started to be great' on p.74). Incidentally, this can also be helpful in relation to other academic tasks such as getting the first and most difficult plan or draft of an essay written, or actually completing a thorough proof-reading or copy-editing of a draft essay.

### Rewards and carrots

Another useful way of seducing yourself into reading something that you have been avoiding is to enter into a contract to complete a particular reading task in a specific period, with the promise of coffee and carrot cake in the wholefood café (or whatever afford-able and easily get at-able reward most takes your fancy) if you are successful.

We both find it helpful to bribe ourselves into undertaking difficult reading tasks. Sometimes we find, as you probably will if you try this approach, that having persuaded ourselves to do a bit of reading by the promise of a reward afterwards (and we don't talk to ourselves all the time by the way) the reading in question becomes so engrossing that we lose track of time. In such situations we often only realize long after the prescribed period is over that we have missed out on the reward because, for example, the café that sells the lemon cake that we crave closed an hour and a half ago. The rewards that you offer yourself need not involve financial outlay, or the risk of putting on weight. One of us habitually reads when he is having a bath. Often, when he has been avoiding a difficult piece of reading, he will decide to do a small section of it when he first gets into the bath, while making a contract with himself that, if he gets it done, he will then complete his time in the bath while reading something he really wants to read – like a bit of the novel he is reading at the moment, or an article in a newspaper or magazine. In this case the pleasure of reading the thing he wants to read is a reward for getting through the more arduous reading task. We are sure that with a little thought you can think of many different ways of rewarding yourself for successful bursts of focused reading.

A variation on this idea is to make the reward and the reading coincide with one another, as it were. For example, one of us used to work on a campus that was adjacent to a supermarket which did a good deal on afternoon teas, and sometimes, when he had a particular piece of reading to do which he couldn't get his head round, he would decide to spend an hour there having afternoon tea while getting the reading task done before leaving for the hour-long drive home. Then he'd go there, have the afternoon tea (but with a cafetière of coffee rather than tea), and get the dreaded and put-off piece of reading done in relative comfort.

If you decide to try out this method of self-bribery, we recommend that you should be as clear as possible about the reading task that you are giving yourself a specific time to accomplish. For example, you might decide to look for the answer to a particular question or questions, to understand an argument, or to 'break the back' of a particularly difficult and complex passage. Remind yourself as you read that the time is allocated to this particular task. At the end of the time it should then be relatively easy to estimate how successful you were. In contrast, after two hours of 'just reading' (as in 'I'm just going to the library to do a bit of reading' which seems to be a curiously common statement among students), what can you say? Perhaps your eyes were focused on the text for 95 minutes and you turned over 55 pages. But did anything pass from those pages into your imagination? And did any significant neural activity go on inside your head while you were 'reading'? Of course, setting yourself a specific reading task (even with the promise of a reward if you accomplish it) does not guarantee that you will actually engage both your brain and the text and attempt to forge a relationship between the two. That is why the discipline of reminding yourself of the task you are attempting to fulfil and keeping yourself focused on it is just as important as any skill you have in extracting ideas, arguments and information from texts, when you are reading as a student.

## Eating elephants – breaking down mammoth tasks

Many academic reading tasks seem daunting because they involve reading and getting to grips with complex ideas and arguments. They need to be broken down into a sequence of easier steps. As a reader, you will first have to decide what these steps will be. This is a personal and creative task and one that can be very enjoyable. There is a joke that goes 'How do you eat an elephant?' (Answer: 'One bite at a time'). Academic texts are like elephants. To consume them, you have to take an incremental approach.

It is nearly always a good idea to skim through texts to get some idea of what they are about, before attempting to read them in a more detailed and systematic way. This is especially important when the text is densely packed with facts or arguments, sloppily written or overladen with jargon and difficult words. It is important to bear in mind that a text might be difficult for you just because it is difficult, so that anyone would find it hard. You should not allow yourself to embrace the idea that if you do not understand – at first, second or even third reading – this necessarily proves that you are thick; it may simply be the case that the author has been unclear in what she has written, or has adopted a more difficult style of writing than is necessary. Barnes (1995: 58) illustrates what we are talking about in the context of a discussion of the range of reasons that might cause you to have problems in understanding a text:

> Sometimes the material you are trying to read holds you back because it is abstract. The topic it deals with is difficult in itself and contains few concrete examples to illustrate the

abstractions. Apart from being abstract, it may contain so many long sentences, or commas, or even sub-clauses, extra details that lose the thread of the beginning of the sentence, additional sub-clauses attempting to creep in, often with irrelevant asides, punctuated with cross-references, so that you need to read it repeatedly before you can understand it (with additional comments added in brackets for extra turgid and boring text) and you become confused, assuming you are still able to concentrate.

## Reading for me and reading for them

Formulating questions to which you want to find answers and creating tasks for yourself, such as listing the main points in an argument, or the key events that are discussed, will allow you to engage with a text more closely. It will also allow you to take control of your reading as *your* work, rather than work you are doing for someone else. Putting your own construction on the process of reading will help to make 'reading for them' into 'reading for me'. This is always a good idea, because it is easier to be motivated about tasks you have set yourself than it is to be motivated about tasks assigned by someone else.

Good luck with your reading at university!

# Examples and possible responses to tasks

## PREFACE AND ACKNOWLEDGEMENTS

'What do Alexander the Great and Winnie the Pooh have in common?' *Answer*: They both have the same middle name.

## PART 2

### Task 2.4: Good and bad reasons for reading as a student

*i Reasons that we think are positive and helpful, that is, those that we think are most likely to lead you to reading that enhances learning.*

To get ideas for essays and assignments.
To expand your knowledge about a subject.
To understand what others have written about topics in which you are interested.
To understand ideas from lectures or seminars, or from other written sources.

To follow up a reference from another source.

To contextualize the views you express in your assignments by showing how they relate to what others have said.

Because you are interested in your topic and you want to know more.

To legitimate or back up what you want to say in an assignment.

Because reading what others have said might cause you to change your mind about a subject.

So that when you come to criticize what others have said, you can do so in an informed way.

For enjoyment – because reading is giving you pleasure.

Because there is a particular piece of information you want or need to find out.

Because your lecturer/tutor wrote the book or article and it might help you understand her views and her research.


*ii Reasons that we consider negative and unhelpful,*
*that is, reasons that we think are less likely to lead*
*to reading that enhances learning.*

So that you can 'drop names' when you are writing assignments.

To give you something to say in your assignments.

Because you think you ought to read this writer, however boring, because she/he is really important and you should refer to her/him in your essay, or think you should, in order to show that you have read her/him. (And anyway, you'll probably get better marks if you do).

Because you paid a lot of money for this set book and want to get your money's worth.

Because your lecturer/tutor wrote the book/article, and it is always good to be able to make a reference to something that your lecturer wrote. (If you think this, turn to what we say about taking care in being accurate with all details of references on pages 142–3).

*iii Reasons that we consider to be neutral, that is,*
*reasons that we do not expect either to lead to or*
*hinder worthwhile work.*

Because lecturers expect to see evidence of reading in essays.

To improve your writing style.

Because a particular book, article, chapter, section, etc., has been
set by a lecturer.

So that when you are writing your assignments you can demonstrate familiarity with what others have written.

Because you've got an exam coming up soon and you'd better
learn something or you'll fail.

To become a better reader.

Because (like cold showers, vitamin pills and green vegetables)
it's good for you.

Because the library will only allow this book out on overnight
loan, and so it must be important.

## PART 3

### *Task 3.2:* Reading for key words

Here are the key words that we spotted in each example:

i   hardness – wood – caused – lignin – cellulose – thickening – cell walls – hardness depending – lignification –
percentage – thick-walled – fibers

ii   whole unnumbered tribe – wooing – plighted lovers –
for him unconscious actors – world-comedy – Love's
contriving – naïve fools – passionately weaving – cords
– strangle passion

iii   principles – paternalism – parties – acknowledge – original position – protect against – weakness – infirmities
– reason – will

iv   Forced – retirement – country cottage, Machiavelli
gambled – boors – inn – returning home – each evening
don – best clothes enter – study – intellectual converse –
great authors – classical Antiquity

v   Gender stereotypes indicate – conversation – men – more
likely – assert, challenge – statements – ignore – while
women – conversation constructively – negotiate – maintain relationships

Did you agree with us? Whether you did doesn't really matter, because the words that strike you as important will relate to your history as a reader, as a learner and as a person.

## Task 3.4: Reading for key words as a way of removing what's unimportant in your written work

Here are the key words in the passage as we saw it:

> most important – feature – literacy hour – all – children working together with – teacher – different parts – focus – texts – different levels – word level – text level – book as – whole – many teachers – not like – got in – way of – important work – now well accepted – varied activities – children – work – group.

How do they compare to the words that you saw as key words?

## PART 6

### Task 6.4: Passage from *The Lopsided Ape: Evolution of the Generative Mind* (p.198)

One fairly extensive study suggests that left-handers, as a group, are not deficient in motor skills. Michael Peters and Philip Servos of the University of Guelph, compared right- and left-handers on a number of manual tests of skill, speed, and strength, as well as on speed of articulation and verbal fluency.[25] They divided the left-handed group into those with consistent and those with inconsistent handedness. In no test were the left-handers, whether of consistent or inconsistent handedness, inferior to the right-handers. However, the inconsistent left-handers were better with the left hand on tests of fine motor skill but better with the right hand on tests of strength – a dissociation that might cause problems in activities requiring both strength and skill.

(Corballis 1991)

### Task 6.5: Passage from *Education and Personal Relationships* (p.31)

It must be stressed straightaway that there is no one skill or even set of skills which a teacher logically must have; rather he requires a very large number of different skills. For example, he requires the humble but important skill of being able to write on the blackboard, or the skill of being able to detect incipient restlessness (or mutiny) in his class. Again, he might be the better of having the skill of the story-teller, or that of being able to see a contemporary application of mathematical ideas or historical events which will make them seem exciting or relevant to his pupils. Clearly this list could be enormously increased, and the good teacher will possess a large number of such skills and will be encouraged to acquire or develop them by colleges of education or headmasters. Different skills or sets of skills in this sense will be required, depending on the subject being taught or the age and stage of the pupil. To stress the multiplicity of skills which the teacher requires is in no way to cast doubt on the claim that teaching is a skill-job, because to characterise a job as a skill-job is not necessarily to say that there is one and only one skill which defines the job. Even musicianship, the paradigm of the skill-job, involves sets of skills. Can we then make any general statements about the sets of skills which are constitutive of the teacher's job?

(Downie, Loudfoot and Telfer 1974)

### Task 6.6: Passage from *The True History of the Elephant Man* (p.20)

Treves's medical career had been associated with the London Hospital from the beginning. He had arrived as a medical student in 1871, become assistant surgeon at the hospital in 1879, and was appointed full surgeon there in 1884. Although he was still only 31, his experience of the appalling range of physical horrors and injuries likely to be admitted into a foundation which existed to administer to the ills of an area which contained some of the worst slums of Europe must have been considerable. It would therefore be reasonable to expect him to be shock-proof, his nose used to such smells as that of gangrene, his eyes accustomed, for example, to the terrible facial injuries which could result from a fight with broken bottles in any London pub on a Saturday night. From what he says, however, it is clear that he was shaken by his first glimpse of Joseph Merrick; and perhaps also taken unawares by his revulsion at the sickening stench given off by Merrick's body. He summed up his initial reaction in one memorable phrase: that Merrick seemed to him 'the most disgusting specimen of humanity'. 'At no time,' wrote Treves, 'had I met with such a degraded or perverted version of a human being as this lone figure displayed.'

(Howell and Ford 1980)

### TREVES'S MEDICAL CAREER AT THE LONDON HOSPITAL

1871...................................................1879..................................................1884

| | | |
|---|---|---|
| arrived as medical student | assistant surgeon | full surgeon |
| Gave off stench | degraded/perverted Version of human being | |

| | | | |
|---|---|---|---|
| Merrick | Disgusting specimen of humanity | Treves | (experienced in horrors and injuries |
| | | | e.g. facial from pub fights) |
| Lone figure | | Revulsion (shaken) | |

## PART 10

### Task 10.3: Passage from conference paper

Here is the passage as it appeared before we prepared it for you to have fun with:

### Resolving the paradox; some suggestions

How can we resolve this paradox – that effective nursing requires closeness and involvement of a kind that leads inevitably to hurt which in turn leads to the risk, to the likelihood even, of less effective nursing?

What could we do in order to recognize and deal with or at least address, the hurt that nurses experience? And why should you do this? Why should you address the problems of hurt in nurses, when resources and care are limited and there are others – patients – who also need your care?

Well one reason might be that because you are caring people, you care about nurses as colleagues, as members of your profession, or maybe just because they are human beings. Another might be the recognition that if nurses are less effective because of hurt, they will be less able to care for the people in their care. In my view since we can't get rid of the risks of hurt without at the same time sacrificing aspects of nursing that are central to its ethos and to its effectiveness, we must attempt to address the hurt that nurses experience. In other words addressing the problems of hurt among nurses might in the end be about caring for patients as much as it is about caring for nurses.

As a result of stress and hurt, nurses need to be supported – they need support of the kind that might be engendered in a co-operative team working closely together. But they need more than this. They need opportunities to share their hurt, to tell it and give it up. Mead (1995b) talks of the way in which she has come to think of the moral and emotional burdens that we suffer as being rather like elephants that we carry around with us. She tells how, during her work with student nurses, she gives them lots of opportunities to share their hurt and upset. Being a good supervisor, she gathers up this upset and hurt (the 'elephants' her students have been carrying about with them). Then having allowed her students to off-load their elephants she takes them home with her; strangely enough I do just the same thing with my student teachers. Unfortunately, as is the case with everyone who is accommodating in the matter of helping others to deal with the elephants they have been carrying round on their head, Professor Mead has to find some way of off-loading the elephants with which she enters home in the evenings. And this is where Mr Mead comes in. How he deals with the elephants to which he is exposed I have yet to discover, but my guess is that being a good husband he begins visibly to bow down under the load as dinner proceeds; something similar is true of Mrs Fairbairn, as I have noticed on the too frequent occasions when I have taken home a particularly heavy load.

Nurses, like everyone else in the caring professions, need to be able to unload the elephants that they are carrying, in a way that does not harm others. And there is a multitude of people whom one might harm by off-loading the stress one has accumulated even in an averagely stressful day: one's spouse, one's friends, one's colleagues, the man who carves us up at the traffic lights when we are hurrying home, one's clients and patients. One way of offering such care and support is clinical supervision, because one of the functions of such supervision must be to enable nurses to survive and grow not only as nurses but as people, because it is only by being personal in their work that they can realize their potential as carers.

And so my view is that nurses who are hurting can be clinic-ally effective but that their clinical effectiveness must be under-pinned by care for them as people. Professionalism in nursing involves not only the application of clinical knowledge and skill combined with the ability to make objective and rational judge-ments, but the ability and willingness to relate as a person, as a real, whole person, to one's patients as whole people. It is be-cause of this that the future of effective nursing lies not only in the continued development of research and in the adoption of wisdom that can be drawn from the results of research, but in the continued development and provision of clinical supervision and support.

# References

You will notice that there are slight differences between the ways in which references in this list are punctuated, and our own preferred style of punctuation, which we discuss on page 139. This results not from inconsistency on our part, but from our need to fit in with the Open University Press house style.

Ahlberg, A. (1984) 'Slow Reader', in *Please Mrs Butler*. Harmondsworth: Puffin.

Barnes, R. (1995) *Successful Study for Degrees*, 2nd edn. London: Routledge.

Beard, R. (1987) *Developing Reading 3–13*. London: Methuen.

Bold, H.C. (1964) *The Plant Kingdom*, 2nd edn. Englewood Cliffs, NJ: Prentice-Hall.

Cahn, Sammy (1955) Love and Marriage, from 'Our Town'.

Corballis, M. (1991) *The Lopsided Ape: Evolution of the Generative Mind*. New York, NY; Oxford: Oxford University Press.

Denscombe, M. (1998) *The Good Research Guide*. Buckingham: Open University Press.

DeSalle, R. and Lindley, D. (1997) *The Science of Jurassic Park and the Lost World – or – How to Build a Dinosaur*. London: HarperCollins.

Dickens, A.G. (1977) *The Age of Humanism and Reformation*. London: Prentice Hall International.

Downie, R.S., Loudfoot, E.M. and Telfer, E. (1974) *Education and Personal Relationships*. London: Methuen.

Fairbairn, G. and Winch, C. (1996) *Reading, Writing and Reasoning: A Guide for Students*, 2nd edn. Buckingham: Open University Press.

Flew, A. (1998) *How to Think Straight: An Introduction to Critical Reasoning*. Buffalo, NY: Prometheus Books.

Fromm, E. (1979) *To Have or to Be?*, 2nd edn. London: Sphere Books.

Hinde, R. (1996) 'Gender differences in close relationships', in D. Miel and R. Dallos (eds) *Social Interaction and Personal Relationships*. London: Sage.

Howell, M. and Ford, P. (1980) *The True History of the Elephant Man*. Harmondsworth: Penguin.

Hunt, G. (1999) 'Abortion: why bioethics can have no answer – a personal perspective', *Nursing Ethics*, 6 (1): 47–57.

Laing, R.D. (1970) *Knots*. London: Tavistock.

McFarlane, J. (1970) *Henrik Ibsen: A Critical Anthology*. Harmondsworth: Penguin.

Maclean, A. (1993) *The Elimination of Morality: Reflections on Utilitarianism and Bioethics*. London: Routledge.

Mair, J.M.M. (1970) 'Psychologists are human too', in D. Bannister (ed.) *Perspectives in Personal Construct Psychology*. London: Academic Press.

Marshall, L. and Rowland, F. (1993) *A Guide to Learning Independently*, 2nd edn. Buckingham: Open University Press.

Nightingale ([1859] 1980) *Notes on Nursing*. Edinburgh: Churchill Livingstone.

Poole, M. (1995) *Beliefs and Values in Science Education*. Buckingham: Open University Press.

Postman, N. and Weingartner, X. (1977) *Teaching as a Subversive Activity*. London: Penguin.

Raban, B. (1982) *Guides to Assessment in Education: Reading*. London and Basingstoke: Macmillan Education.

Rawls, J. (1973) *A Theory of Justice*. Oxford: Oxford University Press.

Rowe, D. (1983) *Depression: The Way Out of your Prison*. London: Routledge and Kegan Paul.

Thomson, A. (1996) *Critical Reasoning*. London: Routledge.

Warburton, N. (1997) *Thinking – A to Z*. London: Routledge.

Williams, K. (1989) *Study Skills*. Basingstoke: Macmillan.

# Index

**WRITING AT UNIVERSITY**
A GUIDE FOR STUDENTS

**Phyllis Creme and Mary R. Lea**

- As a student, what do you need to do to tackle writing assignments at university?
- How can you write more confidently and effectively?
- How can you address the variety of written assignments that you encounter in your studies?

*Writing at University* will make you more aware of the complexity of the writing process. It provides useful strategies and approaches that will allow you to gain more control over your own academic writing. You are encouraged to build upon your existing abilities as a writer and to develop your writing in academic settings through applying a series of practical tasks to your own work. The complete process of writing assignments is considered, including attention to disciplinary diversity, the relationship between reading and writing, the use of the personal, and textual cohesion.

This book is an essential tool to help you develop an awareness and understanding of what it means to be a successful student writer in higher education today.

It will also be invaluable to academic staff who want to support students with their writing.

*Contents*
*You and your university writing – First thoughts on writing assignments – Writing for different courses – Beginning with the title – Reading as part of writing – Organizing and shaping your writing – Writing your knowledge in an academic way – Putting it together – Completing the assignment and preparing for next time – References – Index.*

160pp     0 335 19642 X (Paperback)     0 335 19643 8 (Hardback)

**READING, WRITING AND REASONING (2nd edition)**
A GUIDE FOR STUDENTS

**Gavin Fairbairn and Christopher Winch**

Review of the first edition

> The book's title is absolutely accurate in describing how the authors give the most practical and clear advice on all of the problematic aspects of reading for meaning, developing analytic and coherent thinking and writing in coursework.
>
> This book will be invaluable for any student and it would be sad if most are too busy writing essays and undertaking examination to read it.
>
> *Nursing Times*

If you find writing essays difficult and leave them to the last minute, if you panic as the deadline for submission approaches then this is the book for you. This guide will enable you to develop essential skills in reading, writing and reasoning. The authors are both very experienced in helping students to develop proficiency in these areas. Written in plain language, the book encourages the development of skills in reading and evaluating texts, in the use of a clear and effective writing style and in cogent argument. The practical advice, examples and exercises are invaluable for all students who would like to become better readers, writers and reasoners.

*Contents*
*Part 1: Reading, writing and talking – Talking and writing – What reading involves – What writing involves – Part 2: Writing as a student – Approaches to writing – Technical aspects of writing – Attending to style – Part 3: Developing coherent trains of thought – Influencing the beliefs of others – Arguments of different kinds – Analysing and evaluating arguments – Postscript – References – Index.*

256pp     0 335 19740 X (Paperback)     0 335 19741 8 (Hardback)